D0278970

ANDERSONIAN LIBRARY
★
WITHDRAWN
FROM
LIBRARY
STOCK
★
UNIVERSITY OF STRATHCLYDE

33805 009

THE URUGUAY ROUND

*A Preliminary Evaluation
of the Impacts of the Agreement
on Agriculture
in the OECD Countries*

**Books are to be returned on or before
the last date below.**

-1 JUN 1999 ◇

2 6 JAN 2000 ◇

-9 MAR 2000 ◇

- 6 SEP 2001 ◇

LIBREX—

ORG   NT

ORGANISATION FOR ECONOMIC CO-OPERATION AND DEVELOPMENT

Pursuant to Article 1 of the Convention signed in Paris on 14th December 1960, and which came into force on 30th September 1961, the Organisation for Economic Co-operation and Development (OECD) shall promote policies designed:

— to achieve the highest sustainable economic growth and employment and a rising standard of living in Member countries, while maintaining financial stability, and thus to contribute to the development of the world economy;

— to contribute to sound economic expansion in Member as well as non-member countries in the process of economic development; and

— to contribute to the expansion of world trade on a multilateral, non-discriminatory basis in accordance with international obligations.

The original Member countries of the OECD are Austria, Belgium, Canada, Denmark, France, Germany, Greece, Iceland, Ireland, Italy, Luxembourg, the Netherlands, Norway, Portugal, Spain, Sweden, Switzerland, Turkey, the United Kingdom and the United States. The following countries became Members subsequently through accession at the dates indicated hereafter: Japan (28th April 1964), Finland (28th January 1969), Australia (7th June 1971), New Zealand (29th May 1973) and Mexico (18th May 1994). The Commission of the European Communities takes part in the work of the OECD (Article 13 of the OECD Convention).

Publié en français sous le titre :

LE CYCLE D'URUGUAY

Évaluation préliminaire des conséquences de l'accord sur l'agriculture
dans les pays de l'OCDE

© OECD 1995
Applications for permission to reproduce or translate all or part
of this publication should be made to:
Head of Publications Service, OECD
2, rue André-Pascal, 75775 PARIS CEDEX 16, France.

D
382.41
URU

Foreword

This report begins with a brief history of the process whereby agriculture was incorporated in the Final Act which brought the Uruguay Round of international trade negotiations to a conclusion. The parallel process of stimulating reform of agricultural policies which was undertaken in the OECD in the context of the Ministerial Trade Mandate is also described. The report then details the main elements of the Agreement on Agriculture as they concern the OECD countries and makes a preliminary assessment of the likely impacts on agricultural policy, markets and trade. Particular attention is given to the assessment of the extent to which the agreement will generate agricultural policy reform in the direction of improved market orientation and reduced support to the sector.

The Secretary-General of the OECD agreed to the derestriction of this report, on his own responsibility, as recommended by the Committee for Agriculture at its meeting of 24-27 April 1994. The Council took note of that decision on 28th July 1995.

Table of contents

LIST OF TABLES

LIST OF ANNEXES

LIST OF ANNEX TABLES

LIST OF ANNEX GRAPHS

I. Introduction and background

A. *Objective and scope of the paper*

The objective of this paper is to make an assessment, for the OECD countries, of the trade and agricultural policy implications of the Uruguay Round up to the end of the implementation period in the year 2000. Reflecting OECD's role in the agricultural policy debate over the past decade, the main emphasis in the paper is on the extent to which the Agreement on Agriculture will advance the process of agricultural policy reform. The concept of reform is that envisaged by the objectives set for the Round itself by the Punta del Este declaration and the broader objectives of improved market orientation and resource allocation which have been embraced by OECD governments (OECD 1987a). Attention is also paid to the likely market and trade impacts of the Agreement.

The paper is based on a detailed examination of the Agreement on Agriculture and of the schedules of a selected group of OECD countries. The Agreement on Sanitary and Phytosanitary Measures has also been examined as have other elements of the overall Uruguay Round package which are most relevant to trade in agricultural products. The countries chosen are those for which modules exist in the OECD's Aglink model and, in addition, Switzerland, Iceland and Norway. Mexico is covered but the treatment is less complete than for the other countries. As far as possible, the assessment of the Agreement is guided by the results emerging from the Secretariat's medium term, agricultural outlook process and also draws on other aspects of on-going work in the Secretariat, notably the estimation of Producer and Consumer Subsidy Equivalents (OECD, 1994a). The paper does not attempt to assess implications outside the OECD region. In general, the assessment is carried out with respect to the main, bulk, generic commodities which are the subject of the Producer and Consumer Subsidy Equivalent estimates and of the annual Monitoring exercise and the analysis has not been extended to more highly processed products or to the evaluation of impacts on the up and downstream sectors (OECD, 1994a). This reflects, *inter alia*, the importance of the farm level, primary sector in the agricultural policy reform agenda.

Sweden, Finland and Austria became members of the European Union on 1 January 1995 and aligned their tariffs with the common EC Customs Tariff with effect from that date. This has resulted in increases in bound tariffs for some products across a number of sectors, including agriculture. A W.T.O. Working Party has been set up under Article XXIV (vi) to discuss the question of compensation for these increases in bound rates. Neither has there been agreement on the incorporation of the export subsidy and domestic support commitments of the new EC member states into the schedule of the enlarged EC. In view of the scope of these unresolved issues this paper does not attempt to evaluate the impact of enlargement and the European Community analysis to follow concerns exclusively EC-12.

B. Agriculture in the GATT

Since the GATT's inception, Contracting Parties had not agreed on arrangements which could impose firm discipline on trade in agricultural products. There were several reasons for this, all of which had their roots in the widely held belief that the sector was a declining one which could not be exposed to the full rigours of international competition without causing unacceptable social and economic disruption. The result was a number of general or country specific derogations or exemptions, the combined effect of which was to allow agriculture to be virtually exempted from the disciplines which were applied to trade in industrial products and which had been strengthened through successive rounds of negotiations. Perhaps most important was the explicit exemption of agriculture from the prohibition of export subsidies in Article XVI:3. Although this exemption was conditional on countries respecting "equitable" market shares, such a proviso could not be made sufficiently operational to render it effective and export subsidies proliferated. Important also was the exemption, under Article XI:2(c) which allowed quantitative import restrictions in situations where domestic production was also subject to a quantitative restriction. Canada availed of this Article to maintain quantitative import restrictions in support of its supply management programmes for dairy, poultry and eggs. The United States and Switzerland benefited from country specific derogations. The US waiver freed it from its obligations under Articles II and XI, allowing quantitative import restrictions on any commodity for which a domestic stabilisation or price support policy existed. Switzerland's protocol of accession to the GATT accorded it similar freedom. State trading enterprises operated quantitative import restrictions, and such measures became widespread as in Japan. Only 58 per cent of the agricultural tariffs of the developed economies were bound in the GATT, compared to 78 per cent of industrial tariffs. Finally, mechanisms such as the variable import levies used by the European Community had not been successfully challenged in the GATT up to the time of the launch of the Uruguay Round.

As production increased in many OECD countries under the influence of high domestic prices behind protective barriers, imports from traditional supplying countries were curtailed and export subsidies proliferated. Countries unwilling or unable to engage in export subsidisation lost market share. Agricultural trade became the subject of considerable tensions in international relations and the dispute settlement process of GATT was used increasingly to try to resolve agricultural trade disputes. Of the 82 disputes submitted to the dispute settlement process between 1980 and 1990, 60 per cent concerned agriculture.

C. Agriculture in the Uruguay Round

It was against this background that determined efforts were made to ensure that agricultural trade discipline would be improved as part of the Uruguay Round of international trade negotiations. The Round was launched in 1986 with a mandate from Ministers which became known as the Punta del Este declaration and which stated, inter alia that "Negotiations shall aim to achieve greater liberalization of trade in agriculture and bring all measures affecting import access and export competition under strengthened and more operationally effective GATT rules and disciplines". Moreover, the competitive environment was to be improved "by increasing discipline on the use of all direct and indirect subsidies and other measures affecting directly or indirectly agricultural trade". The major significance of this statement lies in the link created implicitly between domestic support and trade distortions and in the explicit commitment to encompass all direct and indirect subsidies and other measures in the effort to improve the trading environment.

In the period leading up to the launching of the Uruguay Round in 1986 and in parallel with the prepararatory work of the Committee on Trade in Agriculture of the GATT, the OECD had been involved in a major analytical exercise under the terms of its 1982 Ministerial Trade Mandate. This mandate called on the organisation to study, *inter alia*,

"the approaches and methods for a balanced reduction of protection in agriculture, and the fuller integration of agriculture within the open multilateral trading system"

"how best the various objectives of agricultural policies could be achieved in ways compatible with an orderly and improved development of agricultural trade;"

"an examination of relevant national policies and measures which have a significant impact on agricultural trade".

This work resulted, in 1987, in the presentation to ministers of the report "National Policies and Agricultural Trade" and publication of a series of country reports analysing and quantifying the links between domestic agricultural policies and trade (OECD, 1987b). In response, OECD Ministers drew up a set of Principles for a reform of agricultural policy, the text of which is reproduced in Annex 1. These principles again reiterated the link between domestic agricultural policies and trade and outlined a reform agenda, the long-term objective of which was to allow market signals to influence, by way of a progressive and concerted reduction of agricultural support, as well as by all other appropriate means, the orientation of agricultural production. Progress in the direction suggested by the Principles was to be monitored. To that end, an annual monitoring process was initiated which had as one of its main instruments, a measure of the transfers generated by agricultural policies in the form of the Producer and Consumer Subsidy Equivalent (OECD, 1994a). This analytical work proved influential in the development of the agricultural negotiations in the Uruguay Round as the effort to identify and discipline trade-distorting domestic support centred on the Producer Subsidy Equivalent or variants thereof.

The agricultural aspects of the Uruguay Round were developed in the Negotiating Group on Agriculture while parallel technical discussions took place in an especially constituted group known as the Technical Group on Aggregate Measurement of Support and Related Matters. The United States initially proposed the elimination of all domestic support as measured by the Producer Subsidy Equivalent and the retention only of decoupled support i.e. support which is neither production nor trade distorting. The Cairns Group (a group of 14 exporting countries who described themselves as agricultural fair traders) proposed an immediate freeze on price support to be followed by a phased reduction leading eventually to a new set of trading rules for agriculture.[1] The EC tabled a more cautious proposal involving a more modest phased reduction in support to agriculture. "Rebalancing" was a key demand of the Community at this stage and throughout much of the protracted period of discussions which followed.[2] A number of countries were very concerned to gain special treatment in the context of strengthened GATT rules and disciplines for commodities claimed to have a special role in the diet, culture or environment of the country concerned. Japan as an importing country also emphasised the need to have an appropriate balance of rights and obligations between importers and exporters, and argued strongly for the phasing out of export subsidies and for the application of GATT discipline to export restrictions. Developing countries made a strong bid for special and differential treatment and emphasis was placed on the need to minimise the negative impact which significant liberalisation of agricultural trade was thought likely to have on net-food-importing developing countries. More generally, developing countries wished to retain the possibility to foster agricultural development through investment, research and development assistance etc. and argued for cuts in support and protection on a smaller scale and within a longer timeframe.

1.   The Mid-term Review

Given the very wide gap between the negotiating positions of the major players in the Round it proved extremely difficult to reach agreement and the Mid Term Review meeting, originally convened in Montreal in December of 1988, failed to break the impasse. When the Mid Term discussions were resumed in Geneva in April of 1989 agreement was reached on a mid-term package which, under the heading of short term measures, involved a freeze in current domestic and export support and protection levels (GATT, 1989). More explicitly, an undertaking was made not to intensify tariff and non-tariff access barriers, and to freeze support prices to producers. The long term objective of providing for substantial and progressive reductions in agricultural support and protection sustained over an agreed period of time was reiterated. Moreover, the Mid Term Review defined the core elements which were to be encompassed by the Agreement on Agriculture as including quantitative and other non-tariff import access restrictions and tariffs including bindings; internal support measures including income and price support which directly or indirectly affect trade, and direct budgetary assistance to exports, other payments on products exported and other forms of export assistance. These elements later formed the three pillars (import access, export subsidies and domestic support) on which the Agreement on Agriculture was based. The recognition that it would be necessary to proceed separately on the three fronts represented an important shift in emphasis as the Negotiating Group moved away from the discussion of the idea of adopting a single discipline on domestic support which would automatically have repercussions for import access and export subsidisation. Nonetheless, some participating countries, notably the European Community, continued to pursue the idea of a single discipline based on a measure of domestic support. The OECD Council meeting at Ministerial level in June of 1989 endorsed and reiterated the results of the Mid-Term Review in declaring that "Reform should be achieved through mutually reinforcing actions at domestic and international level leading to a fair and market-oriented trading system through substantial, progressive reductions in agricultural support and protection and strengthened and more operationally effective GATT rules and disciplines (OECD, 1989).

Notwithstanding the progress which had been made at the Mid Term Review five more years elapsed before the Final Agreement was concluded. Although agriculture proved one of the most contentious areas, other elements of the Round also proved difficult and contributed to the delay. During the intervening period agreement to the principle that the three elements of import access, domestic support and export subsidies would be separately disciplined, was sought. This period also saw the notion of tariffication, (the conversion of all non-tariff barriers into binding tariffs), first proposed by the United States, gaining currency. However, it was the incorporation of disciplines on export subsidies which proved the most difficult, the EC in particular being reluctant to accept specific limitations. This point was a major factor in the collapse of the meeting held in Brussels in December 1990 to bring the Round to a close although agreement had not at that stage been reached in respect of a special safeguard mechanism – an issue of considerable importance to Switzerland – or in respect of special treatment (exceptions from tariffication) which was of critical importance to Japan. Agreement in principle to accept discipline in each of the three areas of import access, domestic support and export subsidies was not achieved until 1991.

From the end of 1991 onwards the negotiations on agriculture proceeded on the basis of the Draft Final Act which had been put forward by Arthur Dunkel, then Director-General of the GATT. Reflecting proposals on agriculture formulated by Mr. A. de Zeeuw in his role as Chairman of the Negotiating Group on Agriculture, this paper put forward specific quantitative actions and measures designed to strengthen trade disciplines in each of the three areas which, by that date, had been accepted as essential and integral parts of a meaningful agreement on agriculture. Although the EC's proposed reform of its Common Agricultural Policy which was finally agreed in May of 1992 opened the possibility of a solution to the agricultural negotiation, several aspects of the Draft Final Agreement remained problematic. These related to the size of the export subsidy reductions to be undertaken and to whether the compensation payments initiated as part of the EC's CAP reform could be deemed to be sufficiently "decoupled" to remain exempt from reduction commitments in the context of the emerging agreement to reduce the Total Aggregate Measure of Support. These issues proved highly contentious and it was only following protracted bilateral discussions between the US and the EC that an agreement was finally reached.

2. The Blair House Accord

The agreement reached in November 1992 between the US and the EC was known as the Blair House Accord. Although negotiated bilaterally, the main differences from the Draft Final Act were intended to be incorporated into the Final Agreement and this was done, although there were also some elements which remained bilateral and which constitute side agreements to the main Agreement on Agriculture. Consequent changes to the Draft Final Act as proposed by Dunkel are likely to have a significant impact on the outcome of the Round — at least up to the end of the implementation period and possibly beyond — and, for that reason, merit a detailed description.

A smaller reduction in the volume of export subsidies was agreed (21 per cent instead of 24 per cent), relative to the original Dunkel proposal. The "front-loading" mechanism whereby, if the volume of subsidised exports during 1991 and 1992 was higher, on average, than in the 1986-1990 base period, countries were allowed to use the later period as the starting point for reductions was agreed in late 1993 in the context of a further bilateral agreement between the US and the EC, which is sometimes referred to as the second Blair House Accord. The impact of this will be to allow greatly increased subsidised exports during the early years of the implementation period which starts in 1995.

Direct payments under production-limiting schemes were excluded, under certain conditions, from the domestic support reduction commitments during the implementation period of the current Agreement. Measures such as the compensation payments introduced in the context of CAP reform and US deficiency payments, as operated since the 1985 Farm Bill, were thus exempted from the domestic support reduction commitment — although they were not considered as "green" measures (*i.e.* measures exempted on the basis that they are non or minimally trade distorting) under the terms of the original Dunkel proposal.

Finally, a significant change in the AMS discipline was agreed whereby aggregation was allowed. The Blair House Accord also led to the conclusion of a bilateral agreement concerning oilseeds between the US and the EC, which is reproduced in the EC's schedule.

3. The Final Agreement

With these and a number of other important amendments (including Special Treatment, Special Safeguards and the provisions resulting from the second Blair House Accord), the Agreement on Agriculture was finally adopted as part of the Final Act in - December of 1993. Detailed country schedules (detailed offers constituting an integral and legally binding part of the Agreement on Agriculture) were negotiated by the 15th December 1993 and were verified in the months leading up to the Ministerial Meeting in Marrakesh in April 1994. Countries have until the end of 1996 to complete domestic ratification procedures in order to become members of the W.T.O.

II. The main elements of the Agreement on agriculture

The terms of the Uruguay Round agreement are contained in a document entitled the Final Act Embodying the Results of the Uruguay Round of Multilateral Trade Negotiations and the definitive text concerning agriculture is in the section of that document entitled the "Agreement on Agriculture". This text contains commitments in the areas of market access, domestic support and export subsidisation and general provisions concerning monitoring, continuation, etc. In addition, each country's schedule is an integral part of its contractual commitment in the context of the Uruguay Round and is a legally binding document. A third element known as the Modalities for the Establishment of Specific Binding Commitments under the Reform Programme does not now form part of the Agreement. Therefore, aspects which are not fully reflected in the schedules of individual countries but which are described in the Modalities document cannot be used as the basis for dispute settlement proceedings. This is the case, for example, for the minimum access provision whereby countries were to provide tariff quota access opportunities at low or minimal tariff rates beginning at a minimum of 3 per cent of the base period consumption rising to 5 per cent by the end of the implementation period. There is a separate agreement entitled the Agreement on the Application of Sanitary and Phytosanitary Measures. The main terms of the Agreement on Agriculture combined with the "Modalities" and of the SPS Agreement can be summarised as follows.

A. Market access

The main provisions governing market access are contained in Article 4 of the Agreement on Agriculture which refers to concessions contained in country schedules with respect to bindings and reduction of tariffs and to other market access commitments. It also refers to the conversion of non-tariff import measures to ordinary customs duties (usually referred to as tariffication) and defines the only allowable exceptions to the process as those described under the Special Safeguard Provisions (Article 5) and in Annex 5 (Special Treatment). Additional provisions are contained in the Modalities but are only legally binding to the extent that they are also contained in the Agreement or given effect in the schedules. The main provisions can be summarised as follows:

– Convert non-tariff barriers to tariffs based on the difference between average 1986-88 internal prices and world market prices (tariffication).

- Bind all tariffs.
- Reduce all tariffs over 6 years (10 years for developing countries (DCs)) by an average of 36 per cent (24 per cent for DCs) with a 15 per cent (10 per cent DCs) minimum cut per tariff line. Least developed countries are exempt from the reduction commitment.
- Ban on all measures other than ordinary customs duties, the only exceptions being those described under the Special Safeguard Provisions (Article 5) and in Annex 5 (Special Treatment).
- With respect to tariffied commodities current access opportunities to be granted on terms at least equivalent to those prevailing in the base period.
- With respect to tariffied commodities establish minimum access commitments for commodities: the guidelines were 3 per cent of 1986-88 consumption, rising to 5 per cent. The minimum access commitments generally to be established at the 4 digit level of the Harmonised System.
- With respect to tariffied commodities if access was already in excess of the minimum access commitments it was to be maintained and increased. Any increase in current access to be on a most favoured nation basis (m.f.n.) and minimum access opportunities to be implemented as tariff-quotas at low or minimal rates and also on an m.f.n. basis.

Special safeguard provisions

- With respect to tariffied commodities allows for the imposition of additional duties on imports in the event of a surge in imports in terms of volume or a low price based on established trigger levels.

Special Treatment

- Allows countries not to apply tariffication to commodities (which have to be designated in their schedules) on fulfilment of certain conditions, including the granting of minimum access opportunities beginning at 4 per cent of domestic consumption and rising to 8 per cent by the end of the implementation period. (Annex 5)

B. Domestic support commitments

As with the market access provisions the main articles of the Agreement on Agriculture affecting domestic support refer to the schedules and to commitments expressed in them in terms of the Total Aggregate Measure of Support and Annual and Final Bound Commitment Levels. Provisions contained in the Modalities are only legally binding to the extent that they are also contained in the Agreement or given effect in the schedules. The main provisions may be summarised as follows.

16

- Domestic support is to be measured by the "Total Aggregate Measure of Support" (Total AMS), aggregated across all commodities.
- Domestic support that is deemed to be non or minimally trade distorting and direct payments provided through certain production-limiting programmes are not included in the AMS.
- Product-specific support and non-product-specific support which would otherwise be subject to reduction is exempted if it does not exceed 5 per cent of the value of production of the product or of the total value of agricultural production respectively.
- For developing countries, support to encourage agricultural and rural development, investment subsidies, and input subsidies are exempt from the AMS reduction commitments.
- Base Total AMS (referring to the period 1986-1988) to be reduced by 20 per cent in equal annual instalments, with credit granted in respect of reductions which had already occurred during the base period.
- Developing countries must reduce Total AMS by 13 per cent by the year 2005 and the least developed countries cannot exceed Total AMS established in 1986-88.
- Any modification to a domestic support measure or introduction of any new support measure that doesn't satisfy the criteria for exemption shall be included in the Current Total AMS. Notification of all new or modified domestic policies for which exemption is claimed.

C. Export competition commitments

The main provisions concerning export subsidies are contained in the Agreement on Agriculture (Articles 8, 9, 10 and 11) and Annexes and these provisions are given explicit effect in the schedules. As with other aspects of the agreement, the specific implementation details sometimes appear only in the Modalities document and are therefore only legally binding if reflected in the schedules. The main provisions may be summarised as follows.

- Commits Members not to provide export subsidies except in accordance with the Agreement and as specified in Members' schedules.
- Spells out the specific type of export subsidies that are subject to reduction commitments.
- Budget expenditures for export subsidies to be reduced by 36 per cent (24 per cent for DCs) over the six year implementation period (10 years for DCs) from a 1986-90 base. Zero reduction for the least developed countries.
- Quantities exported with subsidies to be reduced by 21 per cent (14 per cent for DCs) over six years (10 years for DCs) from a 1986-90 base.
- Reductions made in equal annual instalments on a commodity-specific basis from the 1986-90 base or from average 1991-92 levels if higher than base period.

17

- Limited flexibility is allowed in phasing in reductions in the second through to the fifth year of the implementation period. The final levels must, nonetheless, reflect full compliance.
- DCs exempt from reduction commitments on subsidies which reduce the marketing costs of agricultural exports and from subsidies on the internal transport and freight of export shipments. [Article 9 (d) and (e)].
- Includes anti-circumvention measures, a commitment to work towards internationally agreed disciplines on export credits and to observe certain practices concerning food aid.
- Under the heading of the prevention of circumvention of export subsidy commitments, food aid should not be tied directly or indirectly to commercial exports and food aid transactions should be carried out in accordance with the FAO "Principles of Surplus Disposal and Consultative Obligations".

D. Export Prohibitions and Restrictions

The main provisions concerning export prohibitions and restrictions are contained in Article 12 of the Agreement on Agriculture and require countries implementing such restrictions to give due consideration to the effects on food security in importing countries, to give advance notice to the Committee on Agriculture and to consult with importers affected by the measure.

E. Sanitary and phytosanitary (SPS) measures

The main provisions concerning the sanitary and phytosanitary measures are as follows:

- Basic rights and obligations: measures taken to protect human, animal or plant life or health, must be based on scientific principles and shall not be applied in a manner that would constitute a disguised trade restriction.
- Harmonization: as far as possible measures shall be based on international standards and guidelines or recommendations where they exist.
- Stricter measures may be introduced or maintained if, based on available scientific information, a Member determines that the international standard does not achieve its appropriate level of protection. In these circumstances the established risk assessment techniques should be employed and the level of sanitary and phytosanitary protection which is deemed appropriate should be decided taking into account the objective of minimising negative trade effects.
- Equivalence: Members shall accept other Members' measures as equivalent if the exporting Member objectively demonstrates to the importing Member that its measures achieve the appropriate level of SPS protection.
- Transparency: Members shall ensure that all changes to SPS regulations are published promptly, provide inquiry point for documents and answers to questions, allow sufficient time for producers in exporting countries to adapt.

– Special and differential treatment: to take account of special needs of developing countries, longer time-frames for compliance to new SPS measures; encourage developing countries to participate in the relevant international organisations.

F. Impacts on agriculture of the World Trade Organisation Agreement

1. Dispute Settlement, Rules and Disciplines

The Final Act which brought together the various agreements reached in the Uruguay Round and provided the charter for the establishment of the World Trade Organisation (WTO) is highly significant in reinforcing the architecture of the world trading system and extending its coverage (OECD, 1994b). Existing multilateral rules, disciplines and enforcement procedures have been strengthened and new areas of international commerce brought into the system. In combination with the specific commitments flowing from the Agreement on Agriculture which are summarised in the above sections, these systemic and institutional changes are likely to reinforce the impetus towards liberalisation of trade in agricultural products and to reduce significantly the uncertainty which has prevailed in the past about the application or enforceability of GATT rules in relation to the sector.

One of the major impacts will come from the improvements to the dispute settlement procedures. Under the new arrangements, dispute settlement will be conducted more efficiently in accordance with pre-determined time limits for each stage of the process; it will no longer be possible for a country to block the process or the adoption of panel reports unilaterally; there will be a right of recourse to an appellate body; and failing settlement or action to bring measures into conformity with obligations under the WTO, retaliatory measures can be authorized by the WTO dispute settlement body in areas covered by WTO agreements. A related benefit, stemming in this case from the Agreement on Agriculture itself, is the Due Restraint provision or "peace clause", which provides a nine year period from the implementation date during which Members will enjoy a degree of protection from legal action in respect of domestic support and export subsidy (but not market access) measures so long as they are in full conformity with their commitments under the Agreement. The corollary of this respite from legal action is the impetus it gives to the conclusion of a further round of negotiations in agriculture which has been accepted under the Agreement and will begin one year before the end of the implementation period for the Agreement and four years prior to the expiry of the "peace clause".

Other areas in which improvements in the general rules and disciplines will have a bearing on conditions for trade in agricultural products include the Agreements on Safeguards and on Subsidies and Countervailing Measures. The Safeguards Agreement now clearly prohibits the application of 'Voluntary' Export Restraints (VERs) and tightens the conditions for application of emergency actions under Article XIX of GATT 1947. The Agreement on Subsidies and Countervailing Measures clarifies the definition of subsidies and divides them into three distinct categories: prohibited, actionable and non-actionable as well as establishing a Permanent Group of Experts to give confidential opinions to any Member country on the nature of any subsidy. Countervailing action rules are consistent in that action may only be taken against a subsidy which is prohibited or actionable and the Agreement sets out details of how to quantify subsidies and injury. While the export subsidy rules under the Agreement on Agriculture effectively exempt domestic support and export measures included under the terms of the Agreement on Agriculture from these more general disciplines during the nine year period specified under the "peace clause", the new general rules and disciplines provide a much firmer basis under the WTO for the future.

Agreements more closely related to the Agreement on Agriculture which are also worthy of note in the context of improving or reinforcing the conditions under which trade in agriculture will occur include the Sanitary Phytosanitary Agreement (which is discussed in more detail in section III.E), and the reconstitution of Plurilateral Trade Agreements on dairy and bovine meat.

2. *Institutional Changes*

A major change arising from the conclusion of the Uruguay Round Agreement is the setting up of the World Trade Organisation, whose functions, structure and *modus operandi* are defined in the Marrakesh Agreement Establishing the World Trade Organisation. One major change is that the new multilateral trading system will operate as a single undertaking. Membership of the WTO implies membership of all its multilateral agreements and the scope for waivers or derogations will be severely restricted, requiring a three-quarters majority in the Ministerial Conference and subject to renewal on an annual basis. This is of particular significance for agriculture, treatment of which in the GATT was characterised by a number of waivers and derogations.

The General Council of the WTO, composed of representatives of all the member countries will discharge the responsabilities of the Dispute Settlement Body and the Trade Policy Review Body. There will also be a Council for Trade in Goods, for Trade in Services and for Trade-Related Aspects of Intellectual Property Rights. The Committee for Agriculture has been assigned the following terms of reference. "The Committee shall oversee the implementation of the Agreement on Agriculture. The Committee shall afford members the opportunity of consulting on any matter relating to the implementation of the provisions of the Agreement." Although notification require-ments have not yet been completely formalised, there is substantial agreement concerning detailed notification formats and timing covering procedures for tariff-quotas, special safeguards, domestic support, export subsidies and export prohibitions. The only aspect of the Agreement on Agriculture which will not be overseen by the Committee for Agriculture concerns tariff concessions which will be dealt with within the framework of the WTO Committee on Market Access. Nonetheless, any member may raise any issue related to tariff concessions in the Committee for Agriculture. There will also be a Committee on Sanitary and Phytosanitary Measures.

III. Implications for agricultural policies and trade in OECD countries

The following sections attempt a preliminary assessment of the importance and significance of the Uruguay Round Agreement for the agricultural sectors in the OECD countries. Attention is paid to both the policy and market implications. Although preliminary, the results are derived from a detailed examination, by the Secretariat, of individual country schedules which has been carried out for the United States, the EC, Japan, Canada, Australia, New Zealand, Switzerland, Iceland and Norway. Where relevant, other elements of the Agriculture Directorate's work such as the annual monitoring exercise, the calculation of Producer and Consumer Subsidy Equivalents and the medium term commodity forecasts, are used in the evaluation of certain aspects of the effects of the Agreement (OECD, 1995b). The assessment relates primarily to the market and policy changes likely to arise over the implementation period of the Agreement, i.e. up to the year 2000. Nonetheless, a distinction is made between potentially important "in principle" or systemic effects of the Round and the measurable changes in trade and agricultural policies likely to occur in practice over the implementation period. These "in principle" changes could transform the multilateral trading system for agriculture. A separate assessment of each of the three pillars of the Agreement is presented first, followed by an overall assessment.

A. Market access provisions

The import access commitments entered into in the Agreement on Agriculture contain a number of elements as explained in the introductory sections of this document. All existing tariffs are to be bound (if not already bound) and reduced and all non-tariff barriers to be converted to tariff equivalents and also bound and reduced (except where Special Treatment is applied). Current and minimum access provisions also apply to these tariffied commodities. It emerges from the sections to follow that the assessment of the significance of the market access provisions depends on the time horizon adopted – with highly significant potential benefits in the longer term but less significant impacts during the implementation period.

1. Tariffication – current and minimum access

a) Terms

With respect to commodities to which tariffication applies, quantitative access commitments under the GATT agreement have been made under two headings. Firstly, countries are expected to maintain current market access opportunities based on the volume of imports during 1986-88 for individual commodities. Secondly, if imports of a specific commodity were not already above 5 per cent of domestic consumption between 1986-88, countries were asked to increase access up to the minimum access opportunity of 3 per cent of the base period domestic consumption starting in 1995, rising to 5 per cent by the year 2000. Access opportunities would, of course, be deemed to exist where the duty resulting from tariffication is low enough to allow the desired level of imports to occur.

The maintenance and, in certain instances, expansion of quantitative market access provisions has two major purposes. The current access provision tries to ensure that exporting countries are not made any worse off, in terms of market access as a consequence of the tariffication process. It has brought the additional benefit, in cases where access had been curtailed since the base period, of restoring base period access opportunities. The minimum access requirement was to help create the opportunity for at least some level of trade for each "tariffied" commodity in each of the signatory countries. This provision was particularly intended to address situations where countries had such a high level of protection that imports of a specific agricultural commodity were effectively prohibited, even after tariffication. It may also prevent a country which used export subsidies on a specific product, and also imported this (or a like) product, from trying to meet its commitment to reduce export subsidies by diverting the product from the export market to the domestic market, thereby displacing imports.

b) Implementation aspects

The fact that the final GATT agreement and associated country schedules do not always include current and minimum access quantities reflects several aspects of the Agreement. The first is that the current and minimum access provisions apply only to tariffied commodities. Secondly, the relevant provisions are contained in the Modalities section and are, therefore, legally binding only in so far as they have been translated into specific commitments detailed in the schedules. Thirdly, the provision does not require a country actually to import a given volume, but rather to establish an access "opportunity". The existence or otherwise of an access opportunity is open to differing interpretations. For example, a country may not have specified quantitative access opportunities in its schedule because it considered that the minimum access opportunity would be available at the bound rate of duty.

Some of the minimum access commitments, as reflected in the Schedules, may incorporate pre-existing or new bilateral arrangements, which, by definition, are offered on a country-specific basis and are, therefore, not consistent with an m.f.n. principle. (Much of the current access commitments is also on a country-specific basis). Moreover, there are a few cases where the in-quota tariffs are little different or not at all different from those resulting from tariffication and applying to over tariff-quota volumes. In other cases, the rates applying to minimum access quantities are higher than those applying to current access quantities while remaining much below over-quota rates. The minimum access opportunities may therefore not fully translate into increased trade.

Another implementation issue raised by the proliferation of tariff quotas under the terms of the minimum access provisions concerns the allocation of tariff quota access opportunities to exporting countries where allocation is not already decided under bilateral arrangements. There are several possibilities available to an importing country. It may grant licenses to domestic importers, in which case most of the rents arising from the tariff quota accrue to the importers. It may allocate licenses to exporting countries in which case most of the rents accrue to the exporter, which, in some cases, may be a government controlled or santioned monopoly export board. Finally, it may auction import licenses and the government of the importing country captures the rents. This method may be most consistent with the m.f.n. principle but attention would need to be paid to the efficiency of the auctioning system and the competitiveness of the domestic market. Moreover, there is uncertainty as to whether auctioning is permissible under GATT rules as it involves a charge which is additional to the bound tariff and which may, therefore, breach GATT bindings. If the allocation of tariff quotas is not implemented so as to be consistent with the m.f.n. principle, the allocation may be subject to challenge under Article XIII of the GATT.

Volume commitments are summarised for a selected group of commodities and countries in Tables 1 to 4, together with the terms governing tariffs and tariffication for the same commodities and countries.

With respect to crop commodities there has been some expansion in access under the minimum access provision. Rice trade is expected to expand by about 1 million tonnes (mostly rice imported into the **Japanese** market and to **Korea** and **Indonesia**) as a direct result of the minimum access provision by the end of the implementation period. The **European Community** has granted new access for 0.5 million tonnes of maize at a maximum tariff of 50 Ecu per tonne and for 0.3 million tonnes of wheat duty-free. **Canada** has granted a tariff quota for wheat of 136 130 tonnes rising to 226 880 by the year 2000. Some specific fruit and vegetable products could also benefit from increased access under this provision.

There will be increased access for dairy products and for various meats. Potentially significant concessions in terms of access opportunities have been granted by the **European Community**. **Switzerland** has granted some increased access on meat, dairy products and potatoes. The **United States** has granted some increased access for dairy products and for beef. Other commodities for the United States were already subject only to tariffs. In the case of beef the restoration of base period access is highly beneficial for Australia and New Zealand. Access to the United States market is unchanged for sugar. For the other countries, imports were often already well in excess of the required 3 to 5 per cent and/or the necessary import opportunity is deemed to exist already for most commodities, and/or tariffication does not apply because a tariff was already the only import measure operative. This is the case for **Japan** with the important exception of rice – a commodity for which Japan has opted to grant minimum access under the Special Treatment provision – and for **Australia** and **New Zealand.** This is also the case for **Canada** for most commodities. Canada has, however, granted increased access for a number of commodities such as turkey, ice cream and eggs or has instituted tariff quotas where imports were prohibited in the past such as butter or margarine. Fluid milk access is limited to consumer cross-border purchases and does not include milk for industrial use. **Norway** already imports a very high proportion of its needs in terms of the major field crops and, hence, has not needed to specify minimum access quantities at preferential tariffs. Tariff quotas have been specified for dairy products where imports in the base period accounted for less than 3 per cent of domestic consumption but the same final, bound tariffs have been specified for in-quota and over quota volumes. The initial in-quota volumes specified for dairy products, meats and eggs are generally less than 3 per cent of base period domestic consumption. **Iceland** has granted significant concessions in terms of imports of livestock and dairy products, commodities for which no imports occurred in the base period. The absolute quantities are small in international terms as the Icelandic market is small. In any case, under current regulations, most meat imports are prohibited for sanitary reasons. With respect to **Mexico,** import concessions already granted in the context of NAFTA have been incorporated into the minimum access commitment with the result that Mexico has had to grant increased access only for milk-powder.

The size of the volume access commitments made by the **European Community** is such as to warrant a more detailed examination. The restoration of the access level which had prevailed during the base period, under a bilateral arrangement, will result in significantly increased access for New Zealand butter into the Community, relative to access in recent years. Under the minimum access provisions the Community schedule incorporates increased access for cheese in excess of 100 000 tonnes. While the in-quota tariffs to apply to these quantities are higher than the preferential tariffs applied to current access quantities they are highly preferential compared to over-quota tariffs. For meat, access commitments have been formulated in terms of an aggregate of different meats with the result that the increased access is concentrated in pigmeat and poultry, although a small additional beef quota is granted at the same, low tariff as applied to current access. In many cases the access quantities reported in the Community's schedule reflect bilateral or plurilateral agreements which were already in place, or which were negotiated in the context of the Uruguay Round itself. For example, import concessions already granted under the Europe Agreements with the countries of Central and Eastern Europe may be incorporated. In some cases, the entire quantity of increased access is already accounted for by these agreements (Tangermann, 1994a). In other cases, additional access opportunities have been created, exploitation of which should allow a freer interplay of competitive forces consistent with m.f.n.

On a country specific basis, the greatest beneficiaries from the current and minimum access provisions among the OECD countries, appear to be New Zealand for dairy products, and Australia for meat and some dairy products. These countries will benefit from the restoration of preferential access at the levels prevailing during the base period under new tariff-quota arrangements operating principally in the United States and European Community markets. The United States and Australia are the OECD countries likely to benefit from increased opportunities to export rice to Japan and Korea.

2. Tariffication — conversion of non-tariff barriers

a) Terms

The Uruguay Round Agreement on Agriculture prohibits the use of non-tariff measures of the kind which have been required to be converted into ordinary customs

Table 1. Market Access Concessions, Commodities subject to tariffication: Selected OECD Countries[1]: Wheat

Country	In-quota				Tariffs/Tariff equivalents			Percentage reduction from base to final bound tariff
	In-quota tariff 1995	In-quota tariff 2000	In-quota volumes 1995	In-quota volumes 2000	Base tariff[2]	Base tariff[3] in *ad valorem* equivalent	MPS[4] in *ad valorem* equivalent	
			000 tonnes					
European Community [5,6]	0	0	300	300	Écu 149/t Écu 231/t	173 % 156 %	107 % 84 %	36 36
Canada [5,7]	C$ 4.41/t	C$ 1.90/t	136.13	226.88	90 % 57.7 %	90 % 57.7 %	23 % 18 %	15 15
Switzerland [8]	SF 350/t	SF 350/t	70	70	SF 890/t	333 %	301 %	15
Japan [9,10]	0 % Y 51 700/t	0 % Y 45 000/t	5 565	5 740	Y 65 000/t	280 %	651 %	15
Norway [11,12]	NKr 2130/t	NKr 2130/t	252	252	NKr 3040/t	507 %	266 %	30
Iceland					350 %	350 %	NA	50
Mexico [13]	50 %	50 %	605	605	US$100	117 %	NA	10

NA = Not Available

Notes:

1. As wheat trade in the United States, Australia and New Zealand was subject to a tariff only regime before the Uruguay Round, these countries are not shown in the table.
2. The base tariff is the initial level of the new bound tariffs resulting from tariffication while the final bound tariff is the maximum which may be applied in 2000 at the end of the implementation period. The actual levels of the final bound tariffs are presented in Annex Tables III.1 to III.10.
3. Where the base tariff is a specific rate or a combination of a specific and an *ad valorem* rate, it has been converted to an *ad valorem* equivalent using an external price from the PSE data base.
4. Unit market price support as measured for the PSE, as a percentage of the external reference price, averaged over the period 1986-1988.
5. The lower row refers to durum wheat while the upper refers to common wheat or wheat other than durum.
6. In the case of the EC the effective constraint in the future is likely to be an arrangement whereby the duty-paid price in the Community should not be more than the intervention price +55 per cent of the intervention price.
7. The over-quota tariff is defined in *ad valorem* terms although with a minimum of C$ 115.98/t in 1995 and C$ 98.5/t in 2000 for wheat other than durum wheat; for durum wheat the corresponding tariff is C$ 97.2/t in 1995 and C$ 82.6/t in 2000.
8. In-quota volumes are set for bread cereals, including wheat.
9. In-quota imports are to be exclusively dealt with by the Food Agency and subject to mark-ups, the maximum value of which is indicated here.
10. Where unit market price support is measured at a wholesale level, the *ad valorem* equivalent is significantly lower at 177 per cent. This reflects the fact that the wholesale price is much lower than the producer price because of government transfers.
11. All wheat.
12. For almost all commodities Norway has specified both an ad valorem and a specific duty: the higher of the two rates will be applied.
13. For wheat Mexico has specified both an *ad valorem* and a specific duty: the higher of the two rates will be applied.

Table 2. Market Access Concessions, Commodities subject to tariffication: Selected OECD Countries[1]: Beef

Country	In-quota tariff 1995	In-quota tariff 2000	In-quota volumes 1995	In-quota volumes 2000	Base tariff[2]	Base tariff[3] in ad valorem equivalent	MPS[4] in ad valorem equivalent	Percentage reduction from base to final bound tariff
			000 tonnes					
United States[5]	US$44/t	US$44/t	656.6	656.6	31.1 %	31.1 %	7 %	15
European Community[6]	20 %	20 %	157	157	20 % / Écu 2 673/t	174 %	90 %	36 / 34
Canada[7]	0	0	76.41	76.41	37.9 %	37.9 %	3.4 %	30
Switzerland[8]	SF 940/t	SF 940/t	22.5	22.5	SF 8 920/t	296 %	250 %	15
Japan[9]	-	-	-	-	93 %	93 %	173 %	46
Norway	NKr 12 150/t	NKr 12 150/t	0.10	1.2	NKr 37 970/t	405 %	144 %	15
Iceland	115 %	-	.057	.095	358 %	358 %	113 %	15
Mexico	-	-	-	-	50 %	50 %	NA	10

Notes:
1. In Australia and New Zealand, beef imports are free of duty and these countries are not shown in the table.
2. The base tariff is the initial level of the new bound tariffs resulting from tariffication while the final bound tariff is the maximum which may be applied in 2000 at the end of the implementation period. The actual levels of the final bound tariffs are presented in Annex Tables III.1 to III.10.
3. Where the base tariff is a specific rate or a combination of a specific and an ad valorem rate, it has been converted to an ad valorem equivalent using an external price from the PSE data base.
4. Unit market price support as measured for the PSE, as a percentage of the external reference price, averaged over the period 1986-1988.
5. This is not applied to Canada and Mexico.
6. This amount includes offals, but excludes live animals.
7. This is not applied to the Unites States and Mexico.
8. In-quota volumes are set for total "red" meat (beef and sheepmeat/lamb).
9. The tariffication of the beef sector in Japan occurred before the conclusion of the Uruguay Round. While the base tariffs reported here are those bound in the Agreement the applied rate in 1995 will be 50 per cent, falling to 38.5 per cent by 2000, a reduction of 59 per cent from the base tariff. The lower tariff was the result of a bilateral arrangement between the United States and Japan, but will apply on an m.f.n. basis.

NA = Not Available

Table 3. Market Access Concessions, Commodities subject to tariffication: Selected OECD Countries[1]: Sugar

Country	In-quota tariff 1995	In-quota tariff 2000	In-quota volumes 1995 (000 tonnes)	In-quota volumes 2000 (000 tonnes)	Base tariff[2]	Base tariff[3] in ad valorem equivalent	MPS[4] in ad valorem equivalent	Percentage reduction from base to final bound tariff
United States[5]	US$31/t US$9/t	US$31/t US$9/t	22.0 1 117.0	22.0 1 117.0	US$421/t US$399/t	216 % N.A.	144 % N.A.	15 15
European Community[5,6]	–	0	1 304.7	1 304.7	Écu 524/t Écu 424/t	274 % N.A.	235 % N.A.	20 20
Canada[5]	–	–	–	–	C$ 41.67/t C$ 32.54/t	16 % N.A.	9 % N.A.	15 15
Switzerland[5,7]	–	–	–	–	SF 720/t	293 %	350 %	15
Australia[5]	–	–	–	–	A$ 140/t	53 %	12 %	50
Japan[5]	–	–	–	–	Y 121 300/t Y 84 500/t	252 % N.A.	184 % N.A.	15 15
Norway[8]	–	–	–	–	NOK 100/t	N.A.	N.A.	70
Iceland	–	–	–	–	350 %	350 %	N.A.	50
Mexico[9]	50 %	50 %	110	184	US$400	206%	N.A.	28

Notes:

1. In Canada, Switzerland, Australia and Japan, sugar was already subject to a tariff - only regime before the inclusion of the Uruguay Round. However, the tariff level is indicated for these countries
2. The base tariff is the initial level of the new bound tariffs resulting from tariffication while the final bound tariff is the maximum which may be applied in 2000 at the end of the implementation period. The actual levels of the final bound tariffs are presented in Annex Tables III.1 to III.10
3. Where the base tariff is a specific rate or a combination of a specific and an *ad valorem* rate, it has been converted to an *ad valorem* equivalent using an external price from the PSE data base.
4. Unit market price support as measured for the PSE, as a percentage of the external reference price, averaged over the period 1986-1988.
5. The upper rows show refined sugar, or refined sugar and raw beet sugar (United States, EC, Switzerland). The lower rows show raw cane sugar.
6. The in-quota volumes are set for cane or beet sugar. 10 000 tonnes are allocated to India and 1 294 700 tonnes to ACP countries in accordance with the provisions of the Lomé Convention.
7. When unit market price support is measured at wholesale level, its ad valorem equivalent is 119 per cent. This is because the wholesale price is lower than the producer price due to the operation of the sugar price stabilisation account.
8. There is no production of sugar in Norway.
9. For sugar Mexico has specified both an *ad valorem* and a specific duty: the higher of the two rates will be applied.
NA = Not Available.

Table 4. Market Access Concessions, Commodities subject to tariffication: Selected OECD Countries[1]: Butter

Country	In-quota tariff 1995	In-quota tariff 2000	In-quota volumes 1995 (000 tonnes)	In-quota volumes 2000 (000 tonnes)	Base tariff[2]	Base tariff[3] in *ad valorem* equivalent	MPS[4] in *ad valorem* equivalent	Percentage reduction from base to final bound tariff
United States	US$123/t	US$123/t	4	7	US$1 813/t	138 %	134 %	15
European Community[4]	Écu 868/t	Écu 868/t	76.7	86.7	Écu 2 962/t	254 %	199 %	36
Canada[5,6]	C$ 2 646/t	C$1 138/t	1.96	3.27	351 %	351 %	199 %	15
Switzerland[7]	SF 200/t	SF 200/t	527	527	SF 19 320/t	1 136 %	1 065 %	15
Japan[8,9]	35 % Y 926 000/t	35 % Y 806 000/t	137.2	137.2	35 % Y 1 159 000/t	657 %	507 %	15 15
Norway	NKr 4 420/t	NKr 4 420/t	.3	.6	NKr 29 640/t	434 %	124 %	15
Iceland	216 %	–	.032	.053	674 %	674 %	362 %	15
Mexico	–	–	–	–	50 %	N.A.	N.A.	25

Notes:

1. As butter in Australia and New Zealand was subject to a tariff only regime or was duty free before the Uruguay Round, these countries do not appear in the table.
2. The base tariff is the initial level of the new bound tariffs resulting from tariffication while the final bound tariff is the maximum which may be applied in 2000 at the end of the implementation period. The actual levels of the final bound tariffs are presented in Annex Tables III.1 to III.10.
3. The calculation of market price support for PSE purposes is done on a whole milk and not on a milk product basis. The *ad valorem* equivalent calculations reported here have been done on the basis of indicative international prices for butter reported in the context of the International Dairy Agreement of the GATT. The domestic prices used to generate the estimate of the price gap are wholesale prices where these are available, or support prices where no wholesale series could be identified.
4. The in-quota tariff reported here is that applying to the New Zealand quota of 76 700 tonnes. Access has been granted for an extra 10 000 tonnes of butter at a tariff of Ecu 948/t. Apart from 3 000 tonnes under the Europe Agreements, this extra quota has not been allocated.
5. Of the quota volumes, 1 200 tonnes for 1995, increasing to 2 000 tonnes for 2000 are allocated to New Zealand.
6. The over-quota tariff is defined in *ad valorem* terms, with a minimum of C$ 4 708/t for 1995 and C$ 4 000/t for 2000.
7. In-quota volumes are set for total milk products in milk equivalent.
8. In the case of Japan, the in-quota import is to be exclusively dealt with by the LIPC, and subject to mark-ups, the maximum values of which are indicated here.
9. In-quota volumes are set for the designated dairy products in whole milk equivalent.

NA = Not Available.

duties, and requires the binding of the resulting tariffs. (Pre-existing tariffs have also all been bound). All tariffs created by the tariffication process, are bound and all tariffs including pre-existing ones are to be reduced by, on average, 36 per cent over the period 1995 to 2000. A small number of exceptions to tariffication have been granted under the Special Treatment provision.

b)   Implementation aspects

Tariffication of non-tariff barriers to agricultural trade is one of the most significant "systemic" achievements of the Uruguay Round (Tangermann 1994a). The resulting tariffs are more predictable and, moreover, they provide a common basis for reductions in future negotiations. However, a number of factors may reduce the immediate trade significance of the discipline. Chief amongst these is the fact that many tariffs have been set at high levels, the highest levels being recorded in the sectors perceived as being the most sensitive. These are also the sectors with the highest initial rates of support as measured by the OECD's PSEs. This is confirmed by Tables 1 to 4 which, in addition to the quantitative access commitments, report the tariffs adopted by a selected group of countries for a number of key commodities that have been the subject of tariffication. These tables also report the results of an exercise undertaken to compare for the period 1986-1988, the levels of protection indicated by the *ad valorem* equivalent of the price gaps (estimated where appropriate, using the PSE price comparisons) with the *ad valorem* equivalents of the new base tariffs. This analysis suggests that, in many cases, a very high level of protection has been accorded to quantities which are outside the tariff quotas. The estimations have been extended and applied to the entire period up to 2000, using price assumptions and projections, drawn from the OECD's medium term outlook. These results are presented in Annex 2. It is important to note, however, that the trade restrictive effects of tariffication at such high rates have been somewhat mitigated, and indeed were intended to be mitigated, by the current and minimum access commitments.

Although many of the tariffs resulting from the tariffication process would appear to have been set at very high levels, several factors need to be taken into account in assessing their likely impact. In some cases, countries will not apply the full tariff recorded in the schedules, so that the new tariffs can be interpreted as representing maxima. For example, the tariff applied by Japan to beef is already significantly lower than that indicated in the schedule, Japan having tariffied its beef import provisions in 1988 and having significantly reduced tariffs since that date. Another example concerns EC cereals (except oats) whereby a bilateral arrangement (which is included in the EC schedule), which limits the duty-paid import price to the intervention price increased by 55 per cent will apply, and will result in a level of protection which is lower in virtually all circumstances than the 149 Ecu per tonne which is the maximum tariff possible according to the schedule. There are many situations in which countries could choose to operate a lower tariff than the maximum bound level. Additionally, the fact that a tariff appears to be very high in absolute terms does not imply that it is necessarily prohibitive. This can only be judged by comparison to the level of the domestic price, which may, in turn, be extremely high. The protective effect of tariffs which have been bound as specific rates, of which there are many examples, could be diluted in a situation of rising world prices, although the opposite is the case when world prices fall. Finally, even if tariffs prove prohibitive in respect of bulk, generic commodities they may not be prohibitive with respect to branded, high quality processed products.

Tariffs are required to be reduced by a simple average of 36 per cent with a minimum of 15 per cent per tariff line. As no weighting system has been imposed, there is a risk that the effect of the cut in tariffs will be weakened (Josling, Tangermann, 1994). For example, it is possible to achieve the average reduction through a combination of deep cuts in tariffs which are already low because the country is a competitive producer of the commodity in question, while applying only the minimum tariff cut to other, less competitive sectors. There are several examples among the countries examined where the tariff cut offered for the commodities with the highest levels of tariff equivalents and the highest levels of support, (as measured by the PSE, for example) has been the minimum permissible.

Annex Tables III.1 to III.10 illustrate the tariffication exercise in some detail. In so far as practicable, the tariff lines which have been included in these tables refer to bulk, generic products corresponding to the type of commodities typically covered by the PSE calculations. These tables confirm that very high tariffs have been set for the over tariff-quota imports, and that, for some countries, the level of tariff cuts applied is highly variable.

In the case of the **United States**, the relatively low tariffs applicable to cereals and oilseeds have been bound and, with the exception of the tariff on durum wheat, will be cut during the implementation period by between 36 and 74 per cent. The tariff on durum wheat is to be reduced by 16 per cent. The sectors which have been tariffied are sugar, dairy, beef, sheepmeat, cotton and peanuts. In all these cases, it has been decided to apply the minimum permissible rate of tariff cut of 15 per cent and relatively high tariffs will continue to be applied at the end of the implementation period.

In the case of the **European Community**, a wide range of sectors has been subject to tariffication. For cereals, although initial tariffs have been set in the region of 140 Ecu per tonne, it seems likely that an alternative provision, negotiated with the United States as part of Blair House, is likely to prevail. Under this provision, the duty will be such that the duty-paid import price of cereals may not exceed the EC intervention price increased by 55 per cent. In the case of beef and sheepmeat the tariffs set are a combination of specific and *ad valorem* elements. The European Community has applied the required average 36 per cent cut almost uniformly across the commodities, the major exceptions being sugar and skim milk powder. Tariffs applying to these sectors will be reduced by 20 per cent. Despite the wide application of the 36 per cent reduction, relatively high tariffs will continue to be applied at the end of the implementation period.

In the case of **Canada**, the sectors subject to tariffication are wheat and wheat products, barley and barley products, dairy, beef and veal, margarine, poultry and eggs.

With the exception of beef and veal the reduction to be applied has been set at the minimum 15 per cent. In the case of beef, Canada will apply the same rate of tariff as the United States with a rate of 30.3 per cent being applied from 1995. This is lower than the rate included in Canada's schedule. In the case of both the United States and Canada beef imports may well occur at the tariffs applied. In most sectors, however, that have been subject to tariffication, relatively high tariffs will continue to be applied at the end of the implementation period.

In the case of **Japan**, the sectors which have been tariffied include wheat, barley, dairy products and pigmeat. Most other grains and oilseeds already enter Japan at low or zero tariffs. The beef sector had already been tariffied in 1988 and tariffs subsequently reduced to 50 per cent. Although it is this level of tariff which has been bound, unchanged over the implementation period, Japan has undertaken to reduce it further to 38.5 per cent. For almost all the other commodities reported in Annex Table III.3, Japan has opted to apply the minimum 15 per cent reduction. As a result relatively high tariffs will continue to apply in many sectors at the end of the implementation period.

Towards the conclusion of the negotiation, agreement was reached on the inclusion of a Special Treatment provision under Article 4:2 and Annex 5 of the Agreement on Agriculture, which allows countries not to apply tariffication for commodities fulfilling certain conditions. This was of considerable importance to Japan and Korea, who have opted to apply it to rice and has also been used by the Philippines and Israël. This provision may be used, if base period imports of a product were less than 3 per cent of domestic consumption, if export subsidies had not been provided, and if effective production restricting measures apply and in the case of a developing country only if the commodity concerned is the predominant staple in the traditional diet. In return, however, except if the specific developing country provision concerning "staple diet" applies, minimum access of 4 per cent of domestic consumption must be granted from the first year of the implementation period, rising by 0.8 per cent of the corresponding domestic consumption each year up to the end of the implementation period. If Special treatment is to be continued after the implementation period of the current agreement then "additional and acceptable" concessions must be granted and these concessions will be determined by negotiation. Unless this occurs, the sector will become subject to full tariffication, while maintaining the existing access, which by then will have become 8 per cent of domestic consumption and will have to apply the tariff which would have prevailed during the 1986-88 base period reduced by at least 15 per cent.

The state trading enterprises which currently control imports of rice, wheat, barley, and dairy products will be maintained during the implementation period, to control rice imports under the Special Treatment provision and in-quota imports of the other commodities. Thus, these imports will continue to be dealt with by governmental or quasi-governmental bodies and mark-ups will continue to apply. Maximum mark-ups have been set at 292, 53 and 950 yen per kg for rice, wheat and butter respectively. With the exception of rice, the maximum mark-ups will be reduced by 15 percent over the implementation period. The maximum mark-up for rice is to remain unchanged. Consumer prices for commodities, import of which is controlled by state trading enterprises are, therefore, unlikely to fall significantly.

Tariffs on most basic agricultural commodities were already very low in **Australia**, and the effect of the agreement on tariff reduction will be to further lower existing tariffs, in many cases. The sugar regime had already been tariffied in place of an import prohibition which had operated during the base period and reductions are being implemented progressively. While the level of the bound tariff at the end of the implementation period is high compared with the currently applied rate, nonetheless the effect of the agreement will be to bind the reform already in place. Specific rate tariffs already existing on dairy products other than cheese are to be converted to *ad valorem* tariffs at the very low level of 1 per cent by the end of the implementation period. The only important product to be tariffied is cheese and in this instance the rate of reduction has been set at the minimum of 15 per cent so that a relatively high tariff will continue to apply at the end of the implementation period.

Tariffs on most basic agricultural commodities were already low or zero in the case of **New Zealand**. The reductions agreed are in the range of 25 to 57 per cent. Because of the virtual absence of non-tariff barriers prior to the Agreement, New Zealand has had to tariffy only a small number of commodities, among them apples and pears.

Tariffication applies to a wide range of basic agricultural commodities in **Switzerland**. With the exception of oilseeds, coarse grains and wool, Switzerland has applied the minimum 15 per cent reduction to all the basic agricultural commodities which have been tariffied. As a result, relatively high tariffs will apply to over-quota trade in all the principal agricultural commodities at the end of the implementation period.

Tariffication has been applied to the whole range of bulk, primary commodities in **Norway**. The rate of reduction to apply to most of the major crop products is in the region of 30 per cent, while the minimum 15 per cent has been applied to most meats and to dairy products. In general, relatively high tariffs will continue to apply at the end of the implementation period.

Tariffication has also been applied to the whole range of agricultural commodities in **Iceland**. The rate of reduction to be applied to crops - many of which are not produced in Iceland - is a uniform 50 per cent. Livestock and dairy products have also been tariffied and the minimum reduction of 15 per cent has generally been applied. As a result, relatively high tariffs will continue to apply even at the end of the implementation period.

Mexico's agricultural tariffs had already been bound at the time of its accession to the GATT in 1986 and these bindings have been carried through to Mexico's schedule. The bound rates — at approximately 50 per cent — are considerably higher than the applied rates, which have been in the region of 10-20 per cent. Reductions from bound rates are, therefore, unlikely to have any trade impact. The reduction required of Mexico is an average 24 per cent with a 10 per cent minimum over a ten year period, reflecting its eligibility for Special and Differential Treatment.

3.   Special Safeguard Provisions

The Special Safeguard Provisions (SSP) may be invoked for commodities which have been subject to tariffication. They apply only to imports over tariff-quota volumes and are designed to prevent disruption on domestic markets due to import surges or abnormally low world prices. They permit additional duties to be imposed in situations where the volume of imports increases beyond a specified trigger level which varies according to the share of the domestic market which is supplied by imports, or in situations where prices fall below some specified trigger level. If the SSP has been invoked in response to a surge in the volume of imports the additional duty may not exceed one-third of the ordinary customs duty in effect for the commodity in question and may only be maintained until the end of the year in which it has been imposed.

In principle, the possibility of invoking the SSP could reduce the likely trade impact of tariffication, renders the tariffication process less transparent than would otherwise be the case and creates the possibility that tariffs will, in effect, be variable (Josling, Tangermann 1994). Nonetheless, the inclusion of this special safeguard provision was important in gaining acceptance for the overall package of market access measures. In practice, because the tariffs which have been set as a result of tariffication are high, it is likely that most of the increased trade during the implementation period will be under the minimum access provisions and hence the SSP will not become relevant.

4. Trade and agricultural policy implications of the market access commitments

Tariffication, in itself, constitutes a major change in the policy environment for the agricultural sector, virtually outlawing recourse to the plethora of measures hitherto used in support of domestic agricultural policy. Countries will no longer be able to initiate quantitative import restrictions, variable import levies, minimum import prices, discretionary import licensing, non-tariff measures maintained through state trading, voluntary export restraints or similar border measures. However, the level at which tariffs have been set and the scale and dispersion of reductions to be undertaken suggest that significantly increased trade flows are somewhat unlikely in the short term beyond those provided for under the minimum access provisions.

The immediate trade and agricultural policy impacts of the market access provisions for agricultural commodities in the OECD countries are likely, therefore, to flow almost exclusively from the volume commitments under current and minimum access. To the extent that the many tariff-quota arrangements embodied in the country schedules include new bilateral or plurilateral arrangements or simply absorb existing preferential access arrangements, their impact on trade flows or domestic agricultural policies will be limited. Existing access has, in some instances, been guaranteed and bound, reducing uncertainty and potentially easing trade tensions. Overall, however, the scope for trade flows to be determined in a more competitive environment for the main temperate commodities produced in the OECD area is limited.

A major objective of the Uruguay Round, in general, and of the Agreement on Agriculture in particular, was increased transparency and predictability in the world trading environment. Although much has been achieved, there is uncertainty surrounding some aspects of the Agreement. It is not yet clear in all cases how countries will allocate the increased access under the new or expanded tariff-quotas although notifications are proceeding. Difficulties could arise concerning the interpretation of what constitutes an access opportunity although the WTO Committee on Agriculture will have a detailed process of notification and review. There is a risk that a growing proportion of trade with the OECD area will occur in the context of bilateral or regional arrangements. Finally, there is some uncertainty concerning the possible operation of the SSP, especially for those countries that did not define their reference prices in their schedules.

Increased imports, where they occur during the implementation period, will exert pressure on domestic supply-demand balances. Where the country granting increased access also subsidises exports of the same or like commodities, which is often the case, the pressures on domestic policy will be reinforced. A more complete assessment which attempts to look at the interactions between, and the combined effects of, the different elements of the agreement will be made in later sections of this paper.

B. Domestic support provisions

The existence of a specific binding commitment on the level of domestic support is arguably one of the most significant and innovative features of the Agreement on Agriculture. This conclusion holds notwithstanding the fact that, in practical terms, the domestic support commitment is unlikely to provoke significant policy change during the implementation period over and above changes which have already been decided or implemented.

1. Total aggregate measure of support — definition

The measure of domestic support which has been adopted for the purposes of the Agreement on Agriculture is defined as "the annual level of support, expressed in monetary terms, provided for an agricultural product in favour of the producers of the basic agricultural product or non-product-specific support provided in favour of agricultural producers in general". The measure is, however, subject to a detailed set of exemptions and exclusions the intent of which is to ensure that reductions apply to those policy measures which, most unequivocally, distort production and trade. The AMS, therefore, mainly includes market price support measures and other measures such as direct payments that provide price support to producers.

The detailed list and characteristics of measures which are exempt from the reduction commitments are given in Annex 2 of the Agreement on Agriculture and are presented in a highly summarised form in Table 5 of this document. These include a wide range of general services (such as training and extension, marketing and promotion, inspection and research), domestic food aid, decoupled income support, government financing of income insurance and income safety net programmes, structural adjustment assistance of various kinds, environmental payments and regional assistance programmes. In addition, product specific support which amounts to less than 5 per cent of the value of production of the product in question and non-product specific support which amounts to less than 5 per cent of the total value of agricultural production of a country are exempted from reduction commitments under the terms of Article 6 paragraph 4 (a) of Part IV of the Agreement on Agriculture. This is usually referred to as the *de minimis* provision. Finally, as a result of a change agreed towards the end of the negotiation in the context of the Blair House Accord, paragraph 5 (a) of Article 6 exempts production-limiting programmes from the commitment to reduce domestic support if

i)   such payments are based on fixed area and yields; or

ii)   such payments are made on 85 per cent or less of the base level of production; or

iii)   livestock payments are made on a fixed number of head.

Moreover, the value of such payments is included in the Base Total AMS on which reduction commitments have been taken but is excluded from the Current Total AMS which will be used to measure compliance during the implementation period.

Annex 3 of the Agreement specifies the method which is to be used to calculate the AMS for an individual commodity. In practice, the measurement is dominated by a price gap derived by comparing domestic administered prices with a fixed external reference price and multiplying the resulting estimate of unit market price support by the level of production. The AMS also includes price related direct payments and non-price related direct payments which are represented in the AMS by the relevant budget outlays. Annex 4 — Calculation of equivalent measurement of support — specifies the procedure to be followed in the case of commodities for which it is not feasible to carry out an AMS calculation. The Modalities document provides that the base period for Total AMS reductions will be the years 1986-1988 and that the final bound level shall be 20 per cent below the base period level, the reductions to be achieved in six equal annual instalments. In order to reflect changes in support occurring after 1986 a credit was allowed. Countries have applied the credit by adopting the 1986 level of AMS as the base period level for a commodity in cases where the 1986 level exceeds the average of the 1986-1988 years. The effect, in many cases, is to significantly inflate the final bound level relative to what it would have been had the 20 per cent reduction been applied to the 1986-1988 average.

2.   *Comparison between the aggregate measurement of support and the Producer Subsidy Equivalent*

Producer Subsidy Equivalents (PSEs) were first estimated by the OECD in the context of the 1982 Ministerial Trade Mandate and subsequently as a key element in the annual monitoring of developments in Member countries in the context of the 1987 OECD Ministerial Principles for agricultural policy reform. The PSE is defined as the "annual monetary transfers to agricultural producers from domestic consumers and taxpayers as a result of agricultural policies". This definition reveals that the AMS and PSE are closely related concepts. Indeed the decision to seek a binding commitment in the area of domestic support in the Agreeement on Agriculture was, in part, the result of ongoing work in OECD. The main similarities and differences between the two measures can be characterised as follows.

The PSE is essentially a measure of transfers resulting from agricultural policies. Although the great bulk of the transfers measured relate to market price support policies, which are the most production and trade distorting, the PSE does not distinguish between different measures in the sense of attributing a weighting which relates to the degree of trade distortion. The AMS, on the other hand, by excluding certain measures from reduction commitments implicitly makes a distinction related to production and trade distortions. The OECD's PSE measure is therefore designed to be a measure of the transfers which arise from the many different instruments of agricultural policy and it seeks to reflect the full range of economic distortion arising from agricultural policies. The GATT AMS measure, by comparison, explicitly seeks to reflect only those policies which are more than minimally trade distorting.

Given that, in the long term, virtually all agricultural policy measures (even lump sum transfers) are likely to influence resource allocation decisions, the choice of instruments to be excluded from reduction commitments is to some extent a matter of judgement. In principle, defining a sub-set of measures which are deemed to be those most distortive of trade is quite a pragmatic procedure the impact of which, in terms of the significance of the resulting bindings, can best be judged with respect to individual measures. A preliminary, qualitative evaluation of the procedures used to identify and define a subset of production and trade distorting measures is attempted in the following sections, which are structured to reflect the current PSE classification system. Graphs III.1 to III.5 in Annex III illustrate the evolution in PSEs and AMS since the 1986-88 base period, for a selected group of commodities and countries.

a) Market price support

Both PSE and AMS support indicators are dominated by the price gap estimates which attempt to capture the transfers that result from policies which implicitly tax consumers by inflating domestic prices through a combination of domestic measures and border measures. In principle, both indicators include this type of policy although, in practice, there are differences in methodology. While the PSE uses observed domestic prices and observed, actual external prices, the AMS uses administered prices and a fixed external price (average 1986-1988).

Fixing the external reference price (and perhaps to a lesser extent the choice of the administered instead of the actual market price) would seem to have been essential to get acceptance in GATT of the AMS indicator. It is not surprising that countries were reluctant to accept commitments based on a measure, the main parameters of which can change as a result of changes in exchange rates, world prices or third country policies. It should not be forgotten, however, that the objective of market orientation, in OECD terms, is to promote responses to, and not to mask, these underlying economic parameters. In the Uruguay Round context, it could be concluded that the AMS preserves the essential features of PSE as an indicator of unit market price support, while

Table 5. **Domestic support: the basis for exemption from the reduction commitments**

	Description	Characteristics
1.	General Policies having no or minimal production or trade distortion effects	Should not involve transfers from consumers or provide price support to producers
2.	Government service programmes – Research – Pest and disease control – Training services – Extension and advisory services – Inspection services – Marketing and promotion services – Infrastructural services – Infrastructural works associated with environmental programmes	
3.	Public stockholding for food security purposes	Should be predetermined targets. Sales and purchases to be at current market prices.
4.	Domestic food aid	Direct provision of food or the means to buy food. Purchases by government to be at current market prices.
5.	Direct payments to producers	As under 1 above.
6.	Decoupled income support	Eligibility to be determined by reference to income or status for a fixed base period unrelated to type or volume of production, factors of production or price other than in the base period. No production required to receive payment.
7.	Income insurance and safety net programmes	– Income loss of at least 30 per cent of gross income – Compensation for less than 70 per cent of actual loss – Related solely to income – Cumulated with disaster payments should not exceed 100 per cent of the loss
8.	Natural disasters	– Only in respect of losses in income, livestock, land or other production factors and should not exceed replacement costs. Should not specify future production – Cumulated with (7) above, should not exceed 100 per cent of the loss.
9. 10.	Structural adjustment assistance – Producer retirement – Resource retirement	Total and permanent – Land for a minimum of 3 years, livestock, permanent withdrawal – No alternatives are specified – Payments unrelated to production, prices or factors of production
11.	Investment aids	– Restructuring or reprivatization – Should not be related to other than base period production or prices – Non-commodity specific
12.	Environmental programmes	– Related to fulfilment of specific conditions including production methods or inputs and shall compensate only for increased costs of compliance
13.	Regional assistance programmes	– Clear criteria of disadvantage – Unrelated to production or prices after the base period other than to reduce production – degressive if related to production factors – Compensate for disadvantage only

Source: GATT 1994. Agreement on Agriculture: Annex 2.

rendering the indicator responsive only to changes in policy and therefore tractable as an instrument of trade reform. It does not reflect, and therefore does not require countries to react to, the actual level of market price support as it evolves over time. Both indicators respond in the same way to changes in the level of production.

A possible drawback in the AMS approach is that market price support has only been measured for products for which administered prices are set. This excludes products where market price support is provided entirely through border measures. (These cases are covered by the provisions on market access). No price support measure is included for beef in the case of the United States or Canada or for wheat in the case of the United States.[3] AMS also in some cases excludes the share of the raw material not used for the production of the products for which administered prices are set (as in the case of the EC where AMS is calculated for butter and skim milk powder only). On the other hand, AMS product coverage is wider than PSE coverage — extending to fruits and vegetables, wine, cotton and tobacco — commodities which have not, to date, been covered by OECD's PSEs.

b)   Direct payments

This category of measure is defined very broadly for PSE purposes, covering all measures which generate direct budgetary transfers to producers without raising consumer prices. The only explicit exceptions recognised within the PSE methodology are payments in respect of permanent or long term withdrawal of resources from the sector or "decoupled" lump sum transfers. On the other hand, the AMS exempts from the reduction commitments a large number of measures which are included in PSE. Chief among these are various government services including marketing and promotion as defined in paragraph 2 of Annex 2, income insurance and income safety-net programmes as defined in paragraph 7, payments for relief from natural disasters as defined in paragraph 8, structural adjustment assistance as described in paragraph 11 and environmental and regional assistance programmes as described in paragraphs 12 and 13 respectively.

Probably most important however, both conceptually and in terms of their impact on the measured level of support, are the exemptions from reduction commitments granted to "production-limiting" programmes under the terms of Article 6 paragraph 5 (a) of the Agreement and described in detail in a previous section. This exemption, which covers mainly US deficiency payments and EC area and headage payments, results in a very large divergence between the current annual PSE and the current annual AMS, while also reflecting a divergence in the evaluation of the extent to which it is considered that such programmes are non or minimally-trade or production distorting. The measures remain linked to production and factors of production and there is usually a requirement to produce the commodity in question. On the other hand, the associated direct payments are based on fixed areas and yields and do not provide a direct incentive to increased production. It is therefore difficult to evaluate their production and trade distorting impacts *a priori*, but they can allow production and trade distortions to persist.

c)   Reductions in input costs

Reductions in input costs figure among those measures considered to distort production and trade and are included in both PSEs and AMS. (There is, however, a specific exemption from the AMS for low-income or resource poor producers in developing countries). Further, the impact of the de minimis provision, whereby a non-commodity specific measure may be excluded provided the total transfers associated with the policies are not in excess of 5 per cent of the total value of agricultural production, has meant that most input subsidies have been exempted from the AMS commitment. This limitation in the coverage of the measure, allows the maintenance of schemes which are potentially highly distorting. However, such schemes are included in AMS, and become subject to the general support reduction commitment, once the 5 per cent of production value is breached.

d)   General services

The PSE includes all general services which deliver assistance to producers even those, such as research and development, whose impacts are indirect. All such measures are excluded from the AMS. Although it could not be claimed that such measures do not affect production and trade in any way, the measures are generally not commodity specific and are somewhat indirect and long-term in their effects.

e)   Sub-national measures

Although the definition of AMS includes such measures, none of the countries examined, with the exception of Canada, has explicitly identified such measures in its AMS. These omissions may result from the de minimis provisions. Sub-national measures are, however, of some importance in PSE terms in some countries.

3.   *The expected impact of the AMS commitments during the implementation period of the Agreement*

a)   Current status of the AMS commitments

An attempt has been made, in varying degrees of detail, to evaluate the policy consequences of the AMS commitments which form part of the country schedules. The first step in this exercise was to ascertain the current status of the Total Aggregate Measurement of Support vis-a-vis the final bound levels which constitute the targets to be reached by the year 2000. The results of this exercise are presented in Table 6. In virtually all cases, the general conclusion emerging is that AMS commitments have already been fully met or will be fully met following only minor, further policy adjustments. A major effect of the AMS commitment, therefore, will be to impose a ceiling on the level of the most trade-distorting forms of domestic support and to make it difficult to reverse changes which had already been decided or implemented unilaterally.

The commitment entered into by the **United States** requires it to reduce its total AMS from the base period level of US$23.9 billion to a final bound level at the end of the implementation period of US$19.1 billion. Deficiency payments accounted for almost US$10 billion during the base period and have been included in the base and final bound commitments. However, they are excluded from the current annual total AMS calculation. The result is a drop in the current Total AMS of such a magnitude that the US need not contemplate any further change in policy in order to meet its AMS commitment. There are, therefore, likely to be virtually no policy changes required in response to AMS commitments in the US during the implementation period of the Agreement.

The base period Total AMS reported for the **European Community** is Ecu 73.5 billion to be reduced to a final bound level of Ecu 61.2 billion by the year 2000. Although agricultural policy parameters in the EC are generally set in Green Ecu, the AMS commitment (and the commitment on tariffs and on the value of export subsidies) are expressed in market Ecu. As there has been a growing divergence between Green and Market Ecus through the operation of the switchover mechanism, with market Ecus having the higher value, the commitments are significantly more constraining in market Ecu terms. For example, an administered price which has been held constant in Green Ecu terms since 1986 has actually increased in market Ecu terms by approximately 12 per cent. The estimated level of the Total AMS in 1993, (although subject to a significant margin of error) suggests that a fall of almost Ecu 11 billion had already occurred by 1993, the first year of implementation of CAP reform. A further reduction in the region of Ecu 1 billion is needed to bring the Community to its final bound level. This reduction should be relatively easily achieved as further price reductions, already decided for cereals, take effect in 1994 and 1995. It would seem, therefore, assuming no significant increases in intervention prices in market Ecus or in production, that the Community should not experience any difficulty in meeting its AMS commitment, given the current and planned policy configuration. Therefore, this aspect of the Agreement is unlikely to induce policy changes beyond those already agreed.

Canada's AMS commitment requires a reduction from the starting level of C $5 376 million to a final bound level of C$ 4 301 million. Canada's AMS in 1993 is estimated to be in the region of C$ 4 078 million which implies that Canada is not expected to have to make substantial policy adjustments in order to reach the final bound level for the year 2000. Policy changes already announced such as the abolition of the Western Grains Transportation Act (WGTA) and the change in emphasis towards income safety net schemes designed to be exempt from reduction commitments, mean that Canada will very easily remain within its final bound level of AMS in the coming years.

Japan's commitment in terms of its total AMS requires a reduction from the starting level of 4966 billion Yen to a final bound level in the year 2000 of 3972.9 billion Yen. The AMS calculation is dominated by rice. As both the administered price of rice and the volume of production have fallen since the base period, the rice AMS has fallen significantly. There has also been a significant fall in the beef AMS as a result of tariffication so that Japan seems to have already achieved its final bound level of AMS with a comfortable margin of security.

The commitment entered into by **Switzerland** requires a reduction in AMS from the base period level of SF 5 321 million to a final bound level in the year 2000 of SF 4 257 million. Given that the level of support tended to increase in the years immediately following the base period, the achievement of this reduction could require significant policy adjustments. Preliminary calculations suggest that policy changes implemented in the most recent years, including changes which permit certain direct payments to be excluded, have already brought Switzerland half-way to meeting its commitments. Further changes will however be required to enable Switzerland to meet its final bound level of AMS in the year 2000 (Swiss government, 1994).

Table 6 . AMS commitments: selected countries

	Units	Base period average 1986-1988	Base [1]	Current level (1993)	Final bound level
United States	Million US$	22 245	23 875	N.A.[2]	19 103
European Community	Billion Ecu	73.53	76.505	62.0[3]	61.204
Canada	Million C$	4 870.4	5 376.3	4 078.2[4]	4 301
Japan	Billion Y	4 335	4 966	<4000[5] (1992)	3 973
Switzerland	Million SF	5 321	5 321	5 076[6]	4 257
Australia	Million A$	590	590	271[7]	472
New Zealand	Million NZ$	360.3	360.3	0 (7)	288.2
Norway [8]	Million NKr	14 311	14 311	NA	11 449
Iceland[9]	Million SDR	163	NA	NA	130
Mexico	Billion MN$	29	29	NA	25

Notes:
1. The base period average plus the difference between the base period average and the 1986 level where the latter is higher, calculated on a commodity specific basis.
2. No detailed estimate is available but the 1993 AMS would be in the region of US$14.0 billion with deficiency payments deducted from the base level and assuming no other change.
3. This is a Secretariat estimate subject to a potentially wide margin or error, due to difficulty in verifying and updating the base period data.
4. Secretariat estimates which include GRIP and NISA payments.
5. Japanese government estimate.
6. Policy changes already decided will bring Switzerland's AMS to SF 4 783 million in 1994 (OECD, Swiss Government estimates).
7. Secretariat estimates.
8. It has not been possible to update the AMS estimates for Norway. However, an approximate estimate based on PSE data (holding reference prices fixed) suggests that total AMS has increased since the base period.
9. Iceland has bound its Total AMS in SDR terms.
NA = Not available.
Source: WTO Country Schedules.
OECD Secretariat estimates.
Government estimates.

Among the OECD countries **Australia** has one of the lowest levels of assistance to the agricultural sector whether measured by AMS or PSE. The Total AMS estimated for 1993 is already less than half of the base period level reflecting the de-regulation and reform efforts which have already been carried out by Australia since the base period. There is, therefore, no need for further policy change in Australia arising from its domestic support commitments.

The depth of policy changes which have occurred in **New Zealand** is such that the AMS, as calculated for the 1986-88 period, has disappeared. As part of an economy wide de-regulation and re-structuring New Zealand had, in advance of the base period, begun to eliminate and dismantle various programmes whose impact had been to support producer prices. The relatively high transfers recorded during the base period reflect government write-offs of the outstanding debts of these Stabilisation Programmes – debts which had been incurred in earlier periods. Other surviving measures are eliminated from the AMS calculation under the de minimis provision. There are, therefore, no further changes to be expected in New Zealand policy arising from the domestic support commitment.

While it has not been possible to update the AMS calculations for **Norway**, an approximate estimate based on the PSE calculations has been prepared for the product specific element of the calculation. While prices for agricultural commodities in Norway rose significantly throughout the second half of the 1980s, they fell subsequently, with the result that, by 1994, the product specific AMS would seem to have changed little from its base period level. However, non-product specific payments would seem to have increased significantly. This suggests that Norway may have to make significant policy adjustments in order to be able to meet its AMS commitment.

Until recently **Iceland** was subject to very high inflation and consequently has bound its AMS, its export subsidy levels and its tariffs in terms of Special Drawing Rights (SDR). While the AMS calculations have not been updated, PSE calculations are available for the entire period and indicate that there has been a very significant drop in asistance to the sector since the 1986-1988 period. If AMS and PSE levels are fairly closely correlated, as seems likely, it is also likely that Iceland has already met its AMS commitment. Therefore, no significant additional policy change is necessary in response to this aspect of the agreement.

The shift to production-neutral direct payments in the form of the Procampo programme is such that **Mexico** has already met its Total AMS commitment, with a large margin of flexibility.

Although the previous paragraphs suggest that in most of the countries examined it will not be necessary to make additional domestic policy adjustments per se in order to adhere to the AMS commitments, policy may nevertheless be adjusted in response to pressures resulting from increased imports under the market access provisions and/or in response to the limitations on the use of export subsidies. Domestic pressures, notably on budgets, may also stimulate policy adjustments.

b)   General evaluation of the AMS commitments

On the basis of the results presented above it would appear that the domestic support commitments seem unlikely to provoke widespread policy adjustments beyond those which have already been implemented or decided. The significance of the domestic support discipline hinges, therefore, on the assessment of the significance of the policy changes which have occurred already. An evaluation has already been carried out in the context of the annual Monitoring exercise, against the criteria established by the Ministerial Principles for the reform of agricultural policies, mainly against the commitment to reduce assistance to the sector (as measured by the PSE) and to move in the direction of increased market orientation. The evaluation of the general thrust of reforming measures undertaken since the elaboration of the Ministerial Principles has been rather qualified (OECD, 1995a).

i)   Annual transfers to agricultural producers, as measured by the PSE, have remained at very high levels and assistance is still dominated by market price support, which is the most distorting form of support. Support mechanisms and   instruments, including border measures, have been retained intact in many countries and reductions in PSEs have been achieved by marginal changes in policy parameters rather than by re-instrumentation.

ii)   Many of the amendments to existing policies have involved production-limiting measures of various kinds. These policies may have brought about improvements in market balances in the short run, but they may not necessarily bring about an improvement in market orientation, they have not usually led to reduced assistance and seem likely to generate significant economic distortions over time. Moreover, technological change may erode their production-limiting impacts in the longer term.

iii) The shift which has occurred in the structure of assistance as measured by the PSE, away from market price support towards direct payments, has not occurred in a context of falling levels of assistance in general, and direct payment schemes remain largely linked to production or factors of production. Little progress has been made in targeting measures to specific needs or in making them less production and trade distorting.

c)   Strengths and weaknesses of the AMS approach

Some other aspects of the AMS commitment support the rather qualified assessment of the related policy changes given above, while other features of the commitment will enhance its significance over time.

Consolidation

The Agreement on Agriculture results in a consolidation or binding of policy changes which had occurred in advance of the completion of the Agreement. Policy changes already decided or implemented have become virtually irreversible, while assistance by commodity, as measured by the AMS, has, in fact, been bound at 1992 levels under the terms of Article 13 (Due Restraint), described in more detail later in this section. In future, this aspect of the agreement could come to be considered as one of its major achievements. Moreover, the criteria for inclusion or exclusion from reduction commitments, emerging from work in the OECD and elsewhere, and being codified in the GATT context, undoubtedly influenced the way in which governments implemented policy change prior to the completion of the Round.

Aggregation

A key feature that limits the role of the AMS as a catalyst for policy change is the aggregate nature of the reduction commitment. This allows countries to meet the overall commitment by adjusting policy in a limited number of sectors while maintaining unchanged regimes in others. This was, nevertheless, probably a key factor generating acceptance of the discipline on domestic support. In the case of the **EC** the AMS commitment will be fulfilled as a result of changes in the composition of assistance to the cereals and oilseeds sectors. On the other hand, assistance, as measured by the AMS itself, may be maintained or increased relative to the base period for some other commodities such as sugar, beef and fruit and vegetables provided 1992 levels are not exceeded. In the **US** case the exclusion of deficiency payments from the current annual AMS means that the final bound level of AMS is easily reached, assistance delivered through measures other than deficiency payments could even be increased, and no reduction in assistance is required in sectors such as dairy and sugar. **Japan's** commitment is met mainly through the administered price and production reductions which have already occurred in the rice sector, reflecting the very large weight of that sector in the overall pattern of assistance. The liberalisation of the beef market has also been significant. It is noticeable, among the countries whose schedules have been examined, that the changes which have occurred could, in some cases, alter relative assistance levels by commodity in such a way as to increase distortion between commodities.

Base period

A further factor which reduces the impact of the AMS commitment over the implementation period is that the base years constituted an historic peak for many commodities and countries. Because of the "credit" in respect of changes in AMS occurring between 1986 and 1988, the actual starting point for the AMS reduction is effectively 1986 in cases where assistance peaked in 1986. Thus, the *de facto* reduction in AMS for many countries, when measured with respect to the 1986-1988 average is less than 20 per cent.

Measurement

A strength of the AMS measure is that it is defined in, and commitments are bound in, nominal terms. Hence, even a modest rate of inflation will act to erode the real value of the support over time and hence will constrain the distortion caused by the remaining policies, although provision has been made for cases of excessive rates of inflation.

Due restraint

Further strength is drawn from the provision contained in Article 13 of Part VII of the Agreement on Agriculture, known as the Due Restraint provision or "peace clause". This provision is commodity specific and renders actionable under Article XVI(i) or Articles 5 or 6 of the Subsidies Agreement any increase in support, as measured by AMS or arising from the "production-limiting programmes", beyond that "decided during the 1992 marketing year". This provision is potentially important since it could curtail the scope for increased support for some commodities, where the Total AMS commitment has already been more than met. In contrast to the other provisions of the Agreement on Agriculture in respect of which the implementation period is a six year period commencing in 1995, the implementation period of the Due Restraint clause is nine years.

4. Policy and trade implications of the domestic support commitment

While we are unlikely to see profound policy change beyond what has already been undertaken as an explicit response to the commitments on domestic support, this aspect of the agreement is, nonetheless, potentially of considerable significance. It has conditioned changes which have already occurred and will profoundly influence future policy developments even if it is not itself the catalyst for policy changes. A ceiling has been placed on the most production and trade distorting forms of assistance, and, because it is defined in nominal terms, this ceiling will become more constraining as even modest inflation erodes its nominal value over time.

The characteristics of measures which may be excluded from the reduction commitment, as laid out in Annex 2, together constitute a blueprint for an agricultural policy which could fulfil certain aspects of the 1987 OECD Ministerial Principles (and which were indeed influenced by those Principles) and could guide policy makers towards a policy framework which is minimally production and trade distorting, which is less costly for consumers, more equitable in its effects on producers and consumers and more targeted to specific needs and problems. It does not, however, ensure a policy mix which will necessarily result in reduced assistance. This is illustrated by the continuing high levels of Producer Subsidy Equivalents for many commodities and countries (OECD, 1995a) and by the sharp divergence which can be observed between PSE and AMS and which is shown for a number of commodities in Graphs 1 to 5 of Annex III. The decision under Article 6.5, to exclude "production-limiting" programmes from the reduction commitment could also have significant implications. In many cases these programmes, although less production and trade distorting than open ended price supports breach a key requirement of "decoupling", as defined in Annex 2, in that production is required in order to be eligible for the payment. Moreover, the measures generate significant transfers from taxpayers to producers.

C.   *Export subsidy provisions*

Acceptance of specific limitations on the volume and value of export subsidies was one of the most contentious issues in the agricultural negotiations and indeed in the Uruguay Round as a whole. Not surprisingly, therefore, it is the export subsidy commitment which is likely to have the most immediate, direct impact on markets and trade.

1.   *Terms*

The terms of the export subsidy commitment eventually incorporated in the Agreement on Agriculture call for a reduction of 21 per cent in the volume and 36 per cent in the value of export subsidies. Where exports in the more recent years were higher, countries could generally choose to base the reductions on the average 1991-1992 export subsidy levels (front-loading provision). Otherwise the base is the 1986-1990 period. The end year values and volumes are to be the same as they would have been had the earlier base period been retained. While this adjustment was important in gaining final agreement to the Uruguay Round package on agriculture, the effect will be to allow the US, (wheat, rice, vegetable oils and eggs), the EC (wheat, cheese, poultrymeat, beef and tobacco) Australia (dairy products) and Canada (wheat, butter) significantly larger quantities of subsidised exports throughout the implementation period, than would have been the case under the original provisions of the DFA. Thus, expected benefits in terms of world market prices or increased market share for non-subsidised exports may be less during the first years of the implementation period than would have been the case if the initial 1986-1990 base period had been retained.

Export subsidies which are subject to reduction commitments include those which are contingent on the incorporation of agricultural products in exported, processed products and there is an explicit requirement that the unit subsidy on an incorporated primary product should not exceed what would have been allowable had the primary product been exported. Specific commitments have been made in terms of the value of export subsidies for incorporated products. In addition, there are specific provisions governing food aid in the article dealing with the prevention of circumvention of the export subsidy commitments. There is also an undertaking to work towards the development of disciplines on export credit guarantees or insurance programmes.

The impact of the export subsidy commitments will differ according to the scope and frequency with which countries have used export subsidies in the past. **Japan** has rarely been an exporter of agricultural commodities and has not been required to make any quantitative undertaking in this area of the agreement. **New Zealand**, also, is unaffected, except to the extent that it is now bound not to introduce export subsidies in the future, as is Japan. The **European Community**, on the other hand, uses export subsidies extensively and is required to cut the volume and value of subsidies across a broad spectrum of agricultural commodities and processed products. **Canada** was required to reduce subsidies under the Western Grains Transportation Act in fulfillment of its export subsidy commitment, but has subsequently decided on the elimination of the programme. Canada is also required to reduce producer financed export subsidies in the dairy sector - skim milk powder is the largest single dairy product to be subject to subsidy reductions. **Australia's** export subsidy commitment falls almost entirely on the dairy sector. In the case of the **United States**, the main impact will fall on wheat, although smaller amounts of other grains are also subsidised. Sales of dairy products from CCC stocks and under the Dairy Export Incentive Programme will also be curtailed and relatively small subsidised sales of other livestock products. In **Switzerland**, dairy products account for a high proportion of all export subsidies and within that category cheese predominates with very high unit subsidies. Export subsidies on potatoes, cattle, some fruits and processed products are also subject to reduction in Switzerland. **Norwegian** exports of meats, eggs, dairy products, fruit and vegetables and honey were subsidised during the base period. As subsidised exports of some commodities rose in subsequent years the "front-loading" provision has been used for beef, cheese, whey powder, fruit and vegetables and honey. While Norway's export subsidy commitments will impose a significant constraint on its own internal policy development particularly for dairy products, the quantities involved are not large in world trade terms. **Iceland** had abolished export subsidies in advance of the conclusion of the Uruguay Round Agreement, although the bindings would permit the reinstatement of subsidies on milk and sheepmeat in the future because such subsidies existed in the base period. **Mexico** is committed to reductions in export subsidies on relatively small volumes of wheat, maize, sorghum, beans and sugar. The reduction requirement is 14 per cent for volume and 24 per cent for expenditures over a ten year period.

The volume commitments, as they affect the main commodities and countries, are summarised in Table 7 while the full details of the value and volume commitments are contained in Annex Tables III.11 to III.18.

2.   *Evaluation of the export competition commitments*

a)   General

The types and characteristics of export subsidies to be disciplined are summarised in Table 8. The list of measures is quite exhaustive, definitions are clear and implementation of the discipline seems less likely to lead to difficulties in interpretation. Commitments are made at a disaggregated level which will reinforce their effectiveness and limit the scope for countries to concentrate actions on less sensitive commodities. The level of subsidised exports had increased since the base period for some countries which gives the reduction commitment increased significance, assessed against current trading conditions in agricultural markets. This is so, in spite of the front-loading provision. There can be no export subsidies on products not subject to reduction commitments, relative to the base period, and no increases from base period subsidies. The adoption of a double discipline on value and volume also constitutes a strength. On the other hand, the adoption of a discipline on export subsidies amounts to the legalisation of such subsidies, a feature of the Agreement which clearly creates an important distinction between the treatment of agricultural goods and the treatment of other kinds of goods for which export subsidies are quite clearly prohibited. The protection from challenge thus accorded to export subsidies is, by the terms of the Due Restraint provision, for a nine year period. Although the value of export subsidies and the volume of permitted, subsidised exports will both fall significantly, the remaining permitted volumes and expenditures could still prove disruptive to international trade in some important agricultural products in the short to medium term. In the longer term trade growth will act to reduce the overall significance of subsidies for agricultural products and a growing share of trade will occur in response to market forces. Export credits are not explicitly disciplined, but WTO members have undertaken to work towards the development of internationally agreed disciplines and to abide by those disciplines once they have been adopted. On the other hand, export promotion and advisory services which are widely available have been excluded from both the export subsidy and domestic support reduction commitments.

b) Policies and trade

The key uncertainties in the assessment of the impact of the export subsidy commitments relate to the extent to which policy changes already underway will result in supply, demand and price adjustments sufficient to fulfil the export subsidy commitments. A related question concerns likely world market price developments and whether these will be in the direction, and of a magnitude, to allow exporters who normally resort to subsidies to export without them. To try to answer these questions the medium term projections concerning production, consumption, trade and world prices which have been recently published, are drawn on. The methodology, status and detailed assumptions which form the basis for these projections are explained in some detail in the recently published Agricultural Outlook 1995-2000 (OECD 1995b). These projections rely on information from OECD member countries concerning the evolution of agricultural policy parameters and future market developments. The Aglink model is then used to integrate this information and to provide a consistent set of global market projections. The current set of projections incorporates the effects of the Uruguay Round in so far as member countries were in a position to indicate the changes in policy parameters which they intended to implement and imports and exports have been constrained to be consistent with the concessions and disciplines governing these aspects. The current set of projections also reflect the impact of reform of the Common Agricultural Policy, the release of land from the Conservation Reserve Programme of the United States from 1996 onwards and more general economic assumptions involving strong growth in the non-OECD countries especially the Dynamic Asian Economies, and some strengthening of growth in the OECD countries. The market and world price projections which are drawn on in the paragraphs which follow result from the combined effect of these and other factors, (world price projections are presented in Table 9). The conclusions drawn are indicative of the possible direction and magnitude of changes in markets and prices given certain assumptions and should be interpreted carefully in this light.

The international **wheat** market has been subject to considerable tensions, with the major players engaging in competitive export subsidisation in order to maintain or increase market share. These subsidies are now disciplined and subject to reduction under the terms of the Agreement on Agriculture. According to the medium term outlook world wheat prices are projected to strengthen significantly up to the end of the implementation period and there will be improvements in the functioning of world markets. These projections are conditioned by strong economic growth both within and outside the OECD area up to the end of the century, and by on-going agricultural policy changes in OECD countries, including CAP reform in the EC, by the release of land from the Conservation Reserve Programme in the United States, and by the impact of the Uruguay Round agreement itself.

Assuming a slow-down in the growth of crop yields, that the set aside programme continues to be effective in reducing the area planted and that internal use for animal feed expands strongly, **European Community** subsidised wheat exports will fall to the levels to which they are constrained by the GATT agreement. However, even if all these conditions are fulfilled there will be some build-up of Community wheat stocks in the medium term suggesting that some further adjustments in cereal policy might need to be

Table 7. **Export competition: volume commitment Summary for selected commodities**

	Unit	Average 1986-90	Average 1991-92	1995	2000	Additionality of front loading 1995-2000
Wheat	Million t					
United States		18.4	21.4	20.2	14.5	7.5
European Community		17	20.3	19.1	13.4	8.0
Canada		11.2	14.5	13.6	8.9	8.5
Coarse grains	Million t					
United States		2.0	–	1.9	1.6	
European Community		12.6	–	12.2	10.0	
Canada		4.6		4.4	3.6	
Oilseeds	Million t					
United States		.2	.7	.6	.1	1.2
Canada		2.2	–	2.1	1.7	
Butter	000 t					
United States		27	47	43	21	51.6
European Community		463	–	447	366	
Canada		4.4	12.5	9.5	3.5	15.8
Australia		49.1	68.7	63.7	38.8	48.8

Table 7. **Export competition : volume commitment**
Summary for selected commodities *(Contd)*

	Unit	Average 1986-90	Average 1991-92	1995	2000	Additionality of front loading 1995-2000
Cheese	000 t					
United States		3.8	4.8	3.8	3.0	0.38
European Community		386	427	407	305	102
Canada		11.5	13.1	12.4	9.1	3.9
Australia		63.1	76.4	72.0	49.9	33.2
Norway		20.5	24.3	23	16.2	9.5
Skim milk powder	000 t					
United States		86	116	108.2	68.2	74.8
European Community		308	–	297	243	
Canada		56.9	–	54.9	44.9	
Australia		85.6	114.0	106.3	67.6	71.1
Milk equivalent						
Switzerland	000 t	78.7	–	75.9	62.2	
Iceland	000 l	4		3.81	3.16	
Beef	000 t					
United States		22	–	21.5	17.6	
European Community		1 034	1 324	1 119	817	363
Poultry meat	000 t					
United States		35	–	34.2	28.0	
European Community		368	470	440	290	255
Sheepmeat						
Iceland	000 t	2.3	–	2.2	1.8	

Source: GATT Country Schedules.
OECD Secretariat.

considered. The projected increase in world prices by the end of the period is not sufficient for the Community to export wheat without the benefit of subsidies, although the difference between domestic and external prices will have narrowed significantly.

The **United States** is projected to increase wheat production and world market share over the medium term as productive capacity expands in response to the release of land from the CRP. This will partly offset the stimulus to world prices coming from strong demand growth in the non-OECD area. US market share will increase and a

Table 8. **Subsidies on exports subject to reduction commitments**

– Direct subsidies, including payments in kind, contingent on export performance

– Sale by government or their agencies of non-commercial stocks at prices below domestic market prices

– Payments financed by virtue of governmental action such as a levy, whether or not there is a charge on the public account.

– Subsidies to reduce marketing costs of exports (other than promotion and advisory services)

– Internal transport subsidies for exports which are more favourable than for domestic shipments

– Subsidies on agricultural commodities for incorporation in exported products

growing percentage of wheat exports will be without the benefit of EEP bonuses as the export subsidy commitment entered into by the US falls predominantly on wheat. The policy adjustments already announced by **Canada** more than fulfill its export subsidy commitment and wheat production is projected to remain more or less stable.

The use of export subsidies has not been as widespread for **coarse grains** as for wheat. The main countries or areas affected by the export subsidy discipline are Canada, which has already announced the elimination of the subsidy concerned, and the European Community. With only a moderate increase in world prices projected, the EC is unlikely to be able to make unsubsidised exports. The same uncertainties as for wheat surround the question concerning the need for further policy changes.

Over the medium term significant improvements are expected in the functioning of international **dairy** markets as production growth slows down in response to policy changes already undertaken and as a result of the export subsidy disciplines (together with improved market access under the current and minimum access provisions). Global demand growth for butter and skim milk powder will continue to be weak. Nonetheless, both butter and smp prices are projected to increase as production declines more than demand. Cheese prices will also increase in spite of higher production because of continued strong demand. These changes, should enable countries such as Australia, the United States and Canada to meet their export subsidy constraints through relatively minor policy changes, some of which are already announced or underway. There is a risk, nonetheless, without some policy adjustment, of a build-up of CCC stocks in the US. Structural shifts which have already occurred in dairy production and consumption should also mean that the European Community will easily meet its export subsidy constraint in butter and skim milk powder. There is, however, some uncertainty concerning cheese. Subsidised exports of cheese from the Community had been rising and the Community has availed itself of the front-loading provision for this product. Moreover, large access opportunities have been created in terms of import access. In this sector, very strong internal consumption growth is necessary in order to meet the export

51

subsidy constraint without resorting to much increased levels of unsubsidised exports (there are already some) or to a cut in quota. Switzerland will need to make significant changes to allow it to respect the export subsidy commitment which predominantly affects cheese. The world price projections for butter, skim milk powder and cheese are such that, although rising prices will result in some narrowing of the gap between internal and external prices, the changes will not be sufficient to close gaps, except perhaps in the case of Australia and for butter in the United States. In order, therefore, to be able to continue exporting, countries, that have used export subsidies in this sector in the past, will by and large continue to do so.

The European Community has been virtually the only subsidised exporter of **beef**. The medium term outlook is for little or no price increase to take place in the Atlantic market. There is, therefore, little or no possibility that the Community may export beef without export subsidies. The outlook for EC production and consumption is such that, even at the maximum permitted level of subsidised export there could be a gradual build-up of Community stocks. This suggests that there is a need to consider further policy adjustments in the beef sector. Neither is there a likelihood of other countries that have subsidised small quantities of beef exports in the past being able to export without subsidies during the implementation period.

Limitations on the subsidised export of **pigmeat** and **poultrymeat** also affect, almost exclusively, the European Community and to a lesser degree, poultry in the United States. Although the volumes of subsidised exports from the EC have been significant, the impact of CAP reform is to reduce input costs in these sectors through its impact on feed-grain prices. This development raises the possibility of increased competitiveness in Community production and the possibility of unsubsidised exports. The world price projections are for a significant increase in pigmeat prices and a smaller, but also significant increase in poultry meat prices. Should these price rises materialise, it will be considerably easier for countries that subsidise exports of these commodities to meet the reduction commitments and there is a strong likelihood that price gaps will be eliminated. It is not envisaged, therefore, that it will be necessary to contemplate specific policy changes in these sectors in response to the export subsidy constraint.

D. The Impact of the Agreement on Agriculture on Processed Agricultural Products.

Although it has not been the subject of a detailed analysis for the purposes of this paper, production of, trade and competition in processed agricultural products seem likely to be significantly affected by the Agreement.

For processed products, as for primary products, benefits will flow both from the systemic changes whereby agricultural trade in general will be subject to clearer and more comprehensive disciplines, thus leading to a reduction in disputes and conflicts and more explicitly from the improved dispute settlement procedures. Processed agricultural commodities have often, in the past, been the subject of retaliatory actions in the context of disputes which originated in a primary product sector. This occurred because of the multiplicity of products which made it easy to identify a group of products meeting the required value specified for retaliation and because it was easy to target branded goods associated with particular countries. (Harris 1994). It is also likely that benefits in terms of an improved trading environment will accrue from the Agreement on Sanitary and Phytosanitary Measures.

With respect to the specific terms of the Agreement on Agriculture itself, it is difficult without a case-by-case, country-by-country analysis to draw general conclusions concerning the magnitude or direction of effects. In particular, it is not known to what extent the degree of liberalisation achieved for highly processed goods in the package of market access provisions is greater than that achieved for primary or semi-processed products.

In so far as the import access provisions are concerned, to the extent that they lead to increased supplies of cheaper raw materials to processing industries in the importing countries, the effects will be beneficial. The outcome will, in part, depend on the allocation mechanisms which will be used. In the longer term, should trade begin to flow more freely over the tariffs which have resulted from the tariffication process, processing industries should benefit substantially.

The domestic support commitments should lead to reduced prices of primary agricultural products although, as we have seen in the earlier sections, such effects will be relatively minor in the short to medium term. The liklihood that the policy constraints contained in the domestic support commitments could lead to increased resort to supply limiting measures of different kinds has been identified as a possible negative impact of the agreement, from the point of view of the processing industries. Limitations on the availability of raw materials could prevent these industries from exploiting economies of scale, and therefore reduce their competitiveness.

As with the primary sector it is likely that it is the export subsidy commitments which will have the most immediate impact on the processing sectors. There is a specific commitment on export subsidies paid in the past on the primary product content of certain processed products and Canada, Switzerland, Norway and the EC have explicit commitments in this respect. The value of such subsidies must be reduced by 36 per cent. Moreover, such subsidies cannot be used for products which were not subject to them in the past. For the processing industries this has the value of clarifying the legal position with respect to such subsidies - they are now legal in a sense which was not clear in the past. On the other hand, the processing sectors must adjust to a reduction in export subsidies which is likely to be much greater than the drop in raw material prices which is likely to result from the domestic support commitments. These assymetries could be increased by the commodity specific nature of the export subsidy commitments in contrast to the aggregate nature of the AMS commitment and, in time, should reinforce the pressure for domestic policy reform. The immediate impact of the export subsidy and market access commitments on processing industries will depend, to some extent, on the mechanisms which are chosen to allocate them . Over the longer term and as the share of processed products in agricultural trade grows, the discipline on export subsidies on incorporated products will become increasingly important.

E.   Sanitary and phytosanitary measures

1.   Introduction

All countries maintain measures to ensure that food is safe for consumers, and to prevent the spread of pests or diseases among animals and plants. These sanitary (human and animal health) and phytosanitary (plant health) measures can take many forms, such as requiring products to come from disease-free areas, inspection of imported products, specific treatment or processing of products, the setting of maximum allowable levels of pesticide residues or permitted use of only certain additives in food.

Since 1948 national food safety, animal and plant health measures which affect trade have been subject to GATT rules.[4] Under Article XX:(b) of the GATT, countries can take measures necessary to protect human, animal or plant life or health, as long as the measures do not cause arbitrary or unjustifiable discrimination among countries where the same conditions prevail, nor are a disguised restriction in international trade.

In the previous round of GATT negotiations an Agreement on Technical Barriers to Trade, often called the Standards Code, was negotiated. Although this agreement was not developed primarily for the purpose of regulating sanitary and phytosanitary measures, it does cover technical requirements resulting from food safety and animal and plant health measures, including pesticide residue limits, inspection requirements and labelling. Member governments have agreed to use relevant international standards. They have also agreed to notify other governments through the GATT Secretariat of any technical regulations which are not based on international standards. The Agreement on Technical Barriers to Trade contains provisions for settling trade disputes stemming from the use of food safety and other technical restrictions.

In the Uruguay Round, therefore, as expressed in the Punta del Este declaration adopted in 1986, Member countries planned to discuss sanitary and phytosanitary measures with the aim of minimising the negative effects of such measures on agricultural trade, taking into account the existing international agreement. As it was envisaged that barriers to agricultural trade would be reduced as a result of the Uruguay Round, governments became more concerned that sanitary and phytosanitary measures might increasingly be used for protectionist purposes.

2.   Agreement on sanitary and phytosanitary measures

The Agreement on Sanitary and Phytosanitary Measures is separate from the Agreement on Agriculture. The aim of the Agreement is to improve operation of GATT Article XX: (b) by making it easier to distinguish between genuine health and safety issues and disguised protection.

The Agreement sets out clearer and more detailed rights and obligations for food safety and animal and plant health measures which affect trade. Countries are permitted to impose only those requirements which are needed to protect human, animal or plant life or health and which are based on scientific principles. A government may challenge another country's food safety or animal and plant health requirements based on evidence which shows that the measure is not justified. For this purpose, reasonable access shall be given, upon request, to the importing Members for relevant procedures where the exporting country is claiming its measure is equivalent or that it has a disease-free area. Countries have to be consistent in their decisions on what is safe food, and in response to animal and plant health concerns. As special attention has been given to developing countries throughout the Uruguay Round negotiations, there are special provisions, such as a longer compliance period, in the Agreement on Sanitary and Phytosanitary Measures, in order to strengthen the sanitary system of the developing countries.

3. Implications of the Agreement

It is rather difficult to assess the implications of the Agreement on Sanitary and Phytosanitary Measures for agricultural trade and international markets. The Agreement does not, or cannot, regulate specific policies in any specific sense. Differences in geographical and sanitary conditions among countries make it difficult to apply uniform sanitary and phytosanitary requirements to products originating from different countries (although this is possible with respect to food safety requirements) and it is difficult to assess on a precise scientific basis, the level of sanitary protection appropriate for importing countries. Therefore, the Agreement on Sanitary and Phytosanitary Measures has established general rather than specific guidelines for government behaviour in the area concerned. The motivation for the Agreement arose from a concern that sanitary and phytosanitary restrictions were being employed as disguised protection measures by importing countries. Moreover, it was feared that with the negotiation of new market access commitments in the Uruguay Round certain countries might even be tempted to strengthen sanitary and phytosanitary restrictions. In practice, the effects of the Agreement depend on the spirit in which governments will implement measures under the new guidelines and on the operation of the strengthened dispute settlement provisions agreed in the Uruguay Round.

With respect to trade disputes, the Agreement could become important when bilateral negotiations fail. In the past, disputes concerning sanitary and phytosanitary measures have often been settled bilaterally rather than multilaterally and this situation will probably continue in the future. Indeed because of the strengthened dispute settlement procedures in general, there may be increased incentives for countries to adopt international standards. However, where countries do not rely on harmonisation or equivalence, but insist on domestic standards, arguing they are based on scientific requirements, there is scope for contention in the evaluation of competing scientific argumentation and evidence. The Agreement leaves scope for interpretation in each individual case and it is likely to be some time before its effectiveness can be assessed.

IV. Overall evaluation

A. *"In Principle" achievements*

The Agreement on Agriculture, completed as part of the Uruguay Round, has the potential to transform the policy and trade environment of the agricultural sector. The disciplines that will apply to the sector explicitly encompass domestic as well as trade policies. This is a highly innovative aspect of the Agreement which responds to the ambition expressed at the very outset of the Round that the trade-distorting domestic policies which were at the root of trade tensions and conflicts should be disciplined. A ceiling has been placed on certain key parameters of domestic agricultural policies, notably on the level of administered prices and on the most production and trade distorting direct payments. Countries are committed to reduce aggregate domestic support as measured by the AMS, to the sector as a whole, and would seem to be somewhat constrained by the Due Restraint clause not to exceed a certain historical level of product specific support. On import access, the minimum access commitment has established the principle that hitherto closed markets should be opened at least to some extent, while tariffication has eliminated non-tariff barriers and replaced them with transparent, bound tariffs which are, in turn, subject to a reduction commitment. Export subsidies have been capped and subject to both a volume and an expenditure reduction commitment and export subsidies may not be introduced for products to which they did not apply in the base period. Strengthened disciplines will apply to export prohibitions and restrictions. The Agreement on Sanitary and Phytosanitary Measures also contains significant potential to resolve some issues which have been a source of trade conflicts in the past. Finally, the improved dispute settlement procedures and strengthened rules governing trade in general constitute a significant achievement with potentially important repercussions for agricultural trade.

Although this paper is concerned almost exclusively with the impacts of the Agreement on selected OECD countries it is clear that the effects in the rest of the world are also potentially crucial for OECD countries. One likely impact relates to the impetus to world agricultural trade likely to arise from increased demand in the non-OECD world. Although estimates differ, the benefits of the agreement in terms of overall economic growth could be of a magnitude to generate significantly increased demand for agricultural and food products from outside the OECD region in the longer term. Also, the adoption or strengthening of disciplines in the different domains covered by the agreement will take on particular significance in the light of the possible accession of countries such as Russia and China in the coming years.

B. Effects on trade and agricultural policies during the implementation period

While the Agreement incorporates a number of highly significant and beneficial systemic changes to the trading system for agricultural products, actual impacts on trade and policy over the implementation period, particularly in the early years, may prove to be modest. This conclusion applies both to the trade effects as they translate into improved access and to the domestic policy effects but less so to the reductions in export subsidies. Towards the end of the implementation period, however, the mutually reinforcing effects of the new rules and disciplines will begin to exert significant pressures for policy reforms. Similarly, tangible results from improvements in the functioning of the agricultural trading system may not materialise immediately, as implementation problems are identified in practice, and monitoring and notification procedures evolve under the auspices of the new World Trade Organisation. This rather qualified assessment of the likely impact of the Agreement over the next six years is derived from a number of factors.

Firstly, because the completion of the Uruguay Round was delayed for many years the base period for reductions is now somewhat distant. Some countries have already engaged in reform efforts sufficient to fulfil or partially fulfil their commitments in some areas of the Agreement. While these unilateral reform efforts were in large part inspired by the expectation of an international agreement, many of the improvements in the trading and policy environment which are required are already in place. On the other hand where trade restrictions had been tightened or export subsidies escalated, the commitments are more biting by virtue of the early base period. Secondly, the level of reduction agreed for the AMS and for export subsidies is relatively modest in absolute terms although the reduction will be reinforced by the impact of even moderate or low inflation. While the average tariff reduction required is significant, its impact has been lessened by the absence of a weighting system and by the fact that the average reduction can be achieved by a combination of deep cuts in pre-existing tariffs (already low in many cases) and smaller cuts in tariffs which have resulted from tariffication. Moreover, the reductions are to be applied to base period parameters which seem, in some instances, to be artificially high. These factors may reduce the potential effectiveness of the Agreement as a catalyst for improved trade or for reform of agricultural policy in the direction of improved market orientation and reduced assistance, both during the course of the implementation period of the current agreement and beyond. Taking all its components together, the trade and policy changes likely to flow from the Agreement on Agriculture can be summarised as follows.

There will be some increased trade flows as a result of the Agreement, principally for rice, dairy products and meats (especially beef in the Pacific market) in response to the creation of certain access opportunities under the current and minimum access commitments. For most commodities, it seems unlikely that there will be significant additional trade flowing over the tariffs applying to over-tariff-quota volumes. Most of the increased imports will occur within tariff-quota arrangements and a high proportion within bilateral or other preferential arrangements within those tariff-quotas. Because some pre-existing access opportunities which are now incorporated in schedules have, in the past, not been fully taken up, it is possible that they will remain under-utilised, particularly during the early years of the implementation period. There will be some significant changes in the impact of export subsidies on international markets and on market functioning as the level of subsidy declines along with the share of exports receiving subsidies. The market likely to be most affected by the export subsidy provision is wheat, reflecting *inter alia* the presence in that market of several countries that have engaged in widespread subsidisation. Market shares are likely to change as the US, Australia and Turkey expand output and EC output growth slows. There will also be improvements in international dairy products markets, notably cheese, in the Pacific beef market, and in pigmeat and poultrymeat markets.

On balance, the impact on world prices of the changes in trade which flow directly from the terms of the Agreement on Agriculture seem likely to be modest. This is not surprising in view of the limited increases in market access, the continued incidence of export subsidies in some markets, and the capacity of some low assistance countries to increase production in response to the new trade opportunities which will occur. The medium term projections carried out by the OECD tend to confirm this hypothesis with projected price increases due to a combination of factors as indicated in Table 9. Although the price changes occurring will be underpinned by the implementation of the WTO agreement they are not the major determinant. Rather, it is the stimulus to demand provided by general economic growth in the non-OECD countries, itself partly due to the economy-wide impacts of the various Uruguay Round agreements, which is the main explanatory factor behind these price projections (François *et al*, 1994). Other factors explaining the price projections include policy changes already undertaken such as CAP reform. Nonetheless, the Agreement on Agriculture may prove to be a major determinant of price developments in the Pacific beef market and in the cheese market in the medium term. Given current knowledge about planned changes in administered prices in the countries examined, the world price projections in general permit the tentative conclusion that price gaps between domestic and world prices seem unlikely to be eliminated for most commodities during the lifetime of the present agreement, although they will be much reduced for grains and pigmeat. This, in turn, suggests that the use of export subsidies will continue.

To what extent therefore can the Agreement on Agriculture be expected to provoke policy changes beyond those already implemented or decided? It is clear that the AMS commitments in themselves are likely to generate only relatively minor further policy adjustments among the countries examined. Moreover, the countries that still need to adjust domestic policies to meet their AMS commitments are not the major players in the markets concerned. It remains, therefore, to attempt to gauge the likelihood that the combined effect of increased imports and reduced subsidised exports will necessitate further policy changes. Again, the detailed examination of the schedules combined with the medium term outlook results provide some guidance here. Pressure points, identified in the medium term outlook projections as stock build up, in situations in which imports and/or exports are constrained by the GATT commitments do emerge — implying a possible need, towards the end of the implementation period, for some further policy adjustments. One such pressure point has been identified for EC beef. Should the

Table 9. World prices, 1990-2000

		Average 1990-93	1993p	1994e	1995	1996	1997	1998	1999	2000
Wheat [1]	US$/t	112	120	122	122	129	138	145	150	153
Maize [2]	US$/t	105	112	98	100	104	107	108	109	110
Soyabeans [3]	US$/t	246	259	187	210	246	235	231	228	229
Beef [4]	US$/kg dw	2.71	2.72	2.45	2.47	2.64	2.65	2.67	2.77	2.93
Butter [5]	US$/t	1 404	1 343	1 329	1 333	1 365	1 404	1 451	1 512	1 603
SMP [6]	US$/t	1 503	1 545	1 591	1 410	1 471	1 586	1 625	1 647	1 780
Cheese [7]	NZ$/t pw	3 808	4 115	3 700	3 501	3 418	3 486	3 569	3 674	3 721
Pigmeat [8]	US$/t dw	1 510	1 430	1 240	1 230	1 450	1 466	1 480	1 540	1 590
Poultrymeat [9]	US$/t	1 181	1 220	1 230	1 210	1 270	1 320	1 350	1 380	1 410

1. Fob wheat export price, Trigo pan, Argentine ports.
2. Fob export price, No. 2 yellow corn, Gulf ports.
3. US soyabeans, cif Rotterdam.
4. Nebraska, choice steers, 1100-1300 lb. lw-dw conversion factor 0.63.
5. Fob export price, butter 82 % butterfat, Northern Europe.
6. Average export price fob, non fat dry milk, extra grade, Northern Europe.
7. Average export price fob, New Zealand.
8. Barrows and gilts, No 1-3, 230-250 lb. Iowa/South Minnesota
9. Wholesale weighted average broiler price, 12 cities.
Source: The Agricultural Outlook: 1995-2000 OECD

projected effects on supply and demand of policy changes which have already been implemented prove to have been overestimated, a number of other sectors such as wheat and dairy could also face the prospect of additional policy changes. Of the countries examined, Switzerland and Norway may need to make significant policy adjustments from the outset of the implementation period and, indeed, Switzerland has already begun to do so, while for some others pressures to adjust could emerge over time as the combined effects of the import access, domestic support and export subsidy bindings become manifest. Over the longer term, the interactive effects of the three main disciplines combined with those aspects of the Agreement which constitute long term strengths — such as the effect of inflation on variables whose values are fixed in nominal base-period values — will intensify the pressure to adopt measures which go in the direction of the long term objective of a substantial and progressive reduction in support and protection. Moreover, the criteria for the definition of non or minimally distorting measures which are contained in Annex 2 are such that governments, while fulfilling the long-term objective, have significant flexibility in the choice of measures available to them in pursuit of goals related to structural adjustment, rural development and environment.

C.   Risks and uncertainties

There are many uncertainties, with the potential to affect significantly the outcome of the Round, both in the medium term context which corresponds to the implementation period and in the longer term. At the time of writing some countries have not yet finalised the specific instruments or mechanisms which they intend to adopt in order to implement the Agreement. Some uncertainty surrounds the arrangements which will be developed for the allocation of tariff quotas. Countries may also need to develop allocation mechanisms in cases in which export subsidies will be rationed. The arrangements adopted will, to some extent, determine whether markets become more competitive with access increasingly determined by market forces, or whether increased trade in agricultural commodities is largely managed.

Examination of the Agreement and of country schedules has revealed a number of ambiguities which may give rise to difficulties in interpretation. Notification and monitoring procedures are being defined and will be implemented by the Committee on Agriculture of the W.T.O. Notwithstanding the Due Restraint Article, there is a wide range of issues affecting the implementation of the Agreement which may need clarification during the implementation period. The implementation of the Sanitary and Phytosanitary Agreement also falls into this category. The outcome on these issues may itself have a strong bearing on the nature and scale of the impacts of the Agreement.

The Agreement on Agriculture incorporates a number of asymmetric disciplines, requiring cuts of differing magnitudes, from different base periods in the three areas which it covers. Moreover, these asymmetries have been increased as technical issues concerning implementation and methodology were debated. Most noticeable is the fact that different reference prices are used in the calculation of tariff equivalents and in the market price support component of the AMS, while it is possible that another set of reference prices may be used in invoking the Special Safeguards Provision. These features of the Agreement have somewhat hindered transparency.

There is considerable uncertainty surrounding the economic effects of some of the policy measures which are admitted under the terms of the Agreement. This is particularly the case concerning the impacts of the production-limiting measures which are excluded from the reduction commitment under the terms of Article 6 para 5 of the Agreement. The measures defined here are clearly not fully decoupled in the sense defined in Annex 2. Yet, Article 6, para 5, may actually encourage countries to adopt production-limiting payments in spite of uncertainty about their production effects, notwithstanding the fact that they move the sector in the direction of increased supply management, that they may not improve market orientation, and that they may impose very high costs on taxpayers. There is also some uncertainty concerning the extent to which the Due Restraint article could operate so as to limit growth in commodity specific support. There is also a risk that the combined effect of the exemptions in Article 6 and in Annex 2 may be to allow the total level of transfers to the agricultural sector, (for example, as measured by the PSE) to remain at existing high levels or even to increase.

The previous paragraphs have indicated a number of uncertainties and unknowns concerning the impact of the Agreement on Agriculture. There is a sense in which the full significance of the Agreement can only be judged in the light of experience during the implementation period. In addition, Article 20 of the Agreement on Agriculture acknowledges that the achievement of the long term objective of substantial, progressive reductions in support and protection resulting in fundamental reform is an on-going process and that a continuing process is necessary toward the long-term objectives. It has, therefore, been agreed that negotiations to continue the reform process will be initiated one year before the end of the implementation period. According to the Agreement factors to be taken into account at that time will include experience in implementing the reduction commitments, the effects of the reduction commitments on world trade in agriculture, non-trade concerns, special and differential treatment of developing countries, the objective to establish a fair and market oriented agricultural trading system and what further commitments will be necessary to achieve the long term objectives of substantial progressive reductions in support and protection.

Notes and references

1. The Cairns Group consists of Argentina, Australia, Brazil, Canada, Chile, Columbia, Fiji, Hungary, Indonesia, Malaysia, New Zealand, Philippines, Thailand and Uruguay.

2. Rebalancing had been a key demand of the European Community throughout the negotiations. By rebalancing is meant the idea that the Community would grant access concessions on cereals only in return for a reciprocal concession allowing it to replace the zero tariff on non-cereal animal feeds which had been bound in an earlier round. This had resulted in imports of non-cereal animal feeds displacing community-grown cereal supplies in community live-stock production.

3. There is a small element of market price support in the base period beef AMS of the United States. This relates to purchases of beef which were made to compensate for the dairy termination programme which had been in operation at that time.

4. Article I of the GATT, the most-favoured nation clause, has always required non-discriminatory treatment of imported products from foreign suppliers, and Article III has required that such products be treated no less favourably than domestically produced goods with respect to any laws or requirements affecting their sale. These rules also apply, for instance, to pesticide residue and food additive limits, as well as restrictions for animal or plant health purposes.

5. These organisations include for food safety, the joint FAO/WHO Codex Alimentarius Commission; for animal health, the International Office of Epizootics; and for plant health, the relevant international and regional organisations operating within the framework of the International Plant Protection Convention.

Bibliography

FRANÇOIS, F.F., McDONALD, B., and NORDSTROM, H. (1994), *The Uruguay Round: A Global General Equilibrium Assessment*. GATT, Geneva.

GATT (1989), MTN.TNC/11 Document presenting the full text of the results of the Mid-Term Meeting.

HARRIS S. A., "The Food Industry Perspective", *Agriculture in the Uruguary Round* (1994), editors Ingersent, K. A., Rayner A. J., and Hire R. C, The MacMillan Press.

JOSLING, T. and TANGERMANN, S. (1994), "The Significance of Tariffication in the Uruguay Round Agreement on Agriculture". Paper presented to the North American Agricultural Consortium Workshop on Canadian Agricultural Policy, Vancouver, Canada, May 14.

OECD (1987a), "Communiqué", PRESS/A(87)27, Paris 13 May.

OECD (1987b), *National Policies and Agricultural Trade*, Paris. Also OECD country studies on Australia (1987), Austria (1987), Japan (1987), the United States (1987), Canada (1987), New Zealand (1987), Sweden (1988), Finland (1989), Switzerland (1990), Norway (1990).

OECD (1989), "Communiqué", PRESS/A(89)26, Paris 1st June

OECD (1994a), *Agricultural Policies, Markets and Trade, Monitoring and Outlook 1994*, Paris

OECD (1994b), *The New World Trading System: Readings*, Paris.

OECD (1995a), *Agricultural Policies, Markets and Trade, Monitoring and Outlook 1995*, Paris.

OECD (1995b), *The Agricultural Outlook, 1995-2000*, Paris.

SWISS GOVERNMENT (1994), "Conséquences de l'accord du GATT pour l'agriculture suisse". Rapport du Conseil fédéral à la Commission de l'économie et des redevances du Conseil national. Berne, juin 1994.

TANGERMANN, S. (1994a), "An assessment of the Uruguay Round Agreement on agriculture". Chapter 15 in OECD (1994b).

TANGERMANN, S. (1994b), "The Uruguay Round Agreement on Agriculture: Some Impacts on Central and East European Countries" AGR/EW/EG(94)26. Paper presented to the Ad Hoc Group on East/West Relations in Agriculture at its meeting of 12-15 September 1994.

Annex I

MINISTERIAL PRINCIPLES FOR POLICY REFORM

The Council of the OECD met at Ministerial level on **12 and 13 May 1987.** The following is the full text of the section on agriculture in the Communiqué issued at the conclusion of that meeting:

"The joint report of the Trade and Agricultural Committees (2) was approved. This important work clearly highlights the serious imbalances that prevail in the markets for the main agricultural products. Boosted by policies which have prevented an adequate transmission of market signals to farmers, supply substantially exceeds effective demand. The cost of agricultural policies is considerable, for government budgets, for consumers and for the economy as a whole. Moreover, excessive support policies entail an increasing distortion of competition on world markets; run counter to the principle of comparative advantage which is at the root of international trade and severely damage the situation of many developing countries. This steady deterioration, compounded by technological change and other factors such as slow economic growth or wide exchange rate changes, creates serious difficulties in international trade, which risk going beyond the bounds of agricultural trade alone.

"All countries bear some responsibilities in the present situation. The deterioration must be halted and reversed. Some countries, or groups of countries, have begun to work in this direction. But, given the scope of the problems and their urgency, a concerted reform of agricultural policies will be implemented in a balanced manner.

"Reform will be based on the following principles:

a) The long-term objective is to allow market signals to influence by way of a progressive and concerted reduction of agricultural support, as well as by all other appropriate means, the orientation of agricultural production; this will bring about a better allocation of resources which will benefit consumers and the economy in general.

b) In pursuing the long-term objective of agricultural reform, consideration may be given to social and other concerns, such as food security, environmental protection or overall employment, which are not purely economic. The progressive correction of policies to achieve the long-term objective will require time; it is all the more necessary that this correction be started without delay.

c) The most pressing need is to avoid further deterioration of present market imbalances. It is necessary:

   – on the demand side, to improve prospects as much as possible inside as well as outside the OECD area;

65

– on the supply side, to implement measures which, by reducing guaranteed prices and other types of production incentives, by imposing quantitative production restrictions, or by other means, will prevent an increase in excess supply.

d) When production restrictions are imposed or productive farming resources withdrawn by administrative decision, these steps should be taken in such a way as to minimise possible economic distortions and should be conceived and implemented in such a way as to permit better functioning of market mechanisms.

e) Rather than being provided through price guarantees or other measures linked to production or to factors of production, farm income support should, as appropriate, be sought through direct income support. This approach would be particularly well suited to meeting the needs of, amongst others, low-income farmers, those in particularly disadvantaged regions, or those affected by structural adjustment in agriculture.

f) The adjustment of the agricultural sector will be facilitated if it is supported by comprehensive policies for the development of various activities in rural areas. Farmers and their families will thus be helped to find supplementary or alternative income.

g) In implementing the above principles, Governments retain flexibility in the choice of the means necessary for the fulfilment of commitments.

"The Uruguay Round is of decisive importance. The Ministerial Declaration of Punta del Este and its objectives provide for the improvement of market access and the reduction of trade barriers in agriculture and will furnish a framework for most of the measures necessary to give effect to the principles for agricultural reform agreed upon by OECD Ministers, including a progressive reduction of assistance to and protection of agriculture on a multi-country and multi-commodity basis. As agreed in paragraph 16 (3), the Uruguay Round negotiations will be vigorously pursued and comprehensive negotiating proposals tabled over the coming months, in this as in other fields. In the Uruguay Round, appropriate account should be taken of actions made unilaterally.

"In order to permit a de-escalation of present tensions and thereby enhance prospects for the earliest possible progress in the Uruguay Round as a whole, OECD governments will carry out expeditiously their standstill and rollback commitments and, more generally, refrain from actions which would worsen the negotiating climate: they will, inter alia, avoid initiating actions which would result in stimulating production in surplus agricultural commodities and in isolating the domestic market further from international markets; additionally, they will act responsibly in disposing of surplus stocks and refrain from confrontational and destabilising trade practices.

"Agricultural reform is not solely in the interests of Member countries. Developing countries which are agricultural exporters will benefit from a recovery on world markets. Developing countries which are importers of agricultural produce will be encouraged to base their economic development on more solid ground, by strengthening their own farm sector.

"Agricultural reform poses vast and difficult problems for Member countries. Strengthened international co-operation is needed to overcome these problems. The OECD will continue to contribute to their solution by deepening further its work; by updating and improving the analytical tools it has begun to develop and which will prove particularly valuable in many respects; by monitoring the implementation of the various actions and principles listed above. The Secretary-General is asked to submit a progress report to the Council at Ministerial level in 1988."

Annex II

BASE PERIOD AND PROJECTED AD VALOREM EQUIVALENT TARIFFS
A COMPARISON OF MARKET PRICE SUPPORT AND THE RATES
RESULTING FROM TARIFFICATION

Annex Table II.1 presents, for a selected group of products and countries, the ad valorem equivalents of the base and final bound tariffs which have resulted from the tariffication process in the Uruguay Round. Where the tariffs resulting from the Uruguay Round are expressed in country schedules in ad valorem terms they are simply reproduced in the table. Where the new tariffs have been set in specific terms or are a combination of specific and ad valorem elements they are converted to ad valorem equivalents. The external world price which is used as the denominator in the estimate of the ad valorem equivalents is usually drawn from, or derived from, the relevant Producer Subsidy Equivalent (PSE) data bases. If no suitable world price was available from this source, alternative series have been used as indicated in the detailed source and methodological notes which accompany this annex. The ad valorem equivalents (AVEs in the table) are then compared to estimates of the market price support accruing to the same products and which, in most cases, correspond to, or are derived from, the estimates of market price support which are contained in the relevant PSE data bases. Again, where no suitable estimate of market price support was available separate calculations have been undertaken and the source and methodological details are given in the detailed notes which accompany this annex. The market price support estimates (MPS in the table) are expressed as ad valorem equivalents using the same external prices as in the calculation of the AVEs. Annex Table II.1 compares the *ad valorem* equivalents (AVE) with the *ad valorem* MPS for the average of the years 1986-1988 which corresponds to the base period used in the tariffication process, as well as the 1999-2000 period which corresponds to the end of the implementation period.

The comparison of the ad valorem equivalents derived from the initial levels of the new bound tariffs for tariffied commodities and those derived from the market price support calculations over similar time periods suggests that the *ad valorem* equivalents of tariffs, as reflected in country schedules provide for a significant additional margin of protection compared to that calculated using the MPS approach. In addition, as the base period represented a peak in terms of domestic prices and a trough in terms of world prices for many countries and commodities, tariffs set with respect to market conditions prevailing during the period are inevitably rather high. Using the same methodology, the analysis has been carried through to the end of the implementation period using assumptions and projections about domestic and world price trends drawn in general from the OECD's medium term outlook exercise (OECD 1995b). Clearly these assumptions and projections are subject to a certain, potentially significant margin of error, and the resulting estimates of the *ad valorem* equivalents of the tariffs and of the level of

67

market price support should be interpreted in that light. Table II.1 presents the comparison of the AVE and the MPS projections, for the average of the years 1999-2000 which corresponds to the last two years of the implementation period of the Agreement on Agriculture. This analysis has been undertaken only with respect to countries for which a module currently exists in the OECD's medium term forecasting model i.e. for the United States, EC-12, Canada, Japan and Australia. (New Zealand is not covered because the tariffication process did not affect it.)

According to the OECD's medium term projections, the implementation period of the Uruguay Round will be characterised, in general, by constant or slightly falling domestic prices for the main agricultural commodities, and by rising world prices. Rising world prices combined with the tariff reductions — a minimum of 15 per cent for each product — act together to reduce the *ad valorem* equivalents of the final bound tariffs and this effect is most noticeable for commodities whose prices are projected to rise significantly and/or those subject to the steepest tariff cuts. Thus, for example, the ad valorem equivalents of the tariffs on wheat, sugar, butter and skim milk powder are projected to fall significantly by the year 2000. Constant or falling domestic prices combined with rising world prices also act, over the implementation period, to reduce the rate of market price support. It is noticeable that there are many examples where the reduction in market price support is sharper than the reduction in the tariffs. According to the projected price trends, market price support should be eliminated for Canadian wheat, for butter in the United States and for beef in the United States and Canada, but, in fact, these countries retain tariff protection on these commodities at the end of the implementation period. In most other cases, a significant margin persists between the ad valorem equivalent of the projected market price support and the higher *ad valorem* equivalents of the tariffs. These results suggest that, for the commodities and countries analysed, the tariff-quotas, rather than the tariffs, will continue to constitute the effective, binding constraint on import access over the implementation period, notwithstanding the fact that the *ad valorem* equivalents of the final bound tariffs will be much lower than their initial levels.

Annex Table II.1
Ad valorem equivalents of base and bound tariffs:
Comparison to the ad valorem equivalent of unit market price support
Selected Commodities, Countries (%)

		1986-1988	1999-2000[5]
WHEAT			
US	AVE	9	3
	MPS	20	7
EC-12[1]	AVE	173	92
	INT+55%/AVE	266	69
	MPS	107	16
Canada	AVE	90	77
	MPS	23	0
Japan[2]	AVE	279	275
	MPS	177	118
SUGAR[3]			
US	AVE	216	109
	MPS	144	40
EC-12	AVE	274	125
	MPS	235	93
BUTTER[4]			
US	AVE	138	81
	MPS	134	0
EC-12	AVE	254	148
	MPS	199	132
Canada	AVE	351	303
	MPS	191	93
Japan	AVE	657	574
	MPS	507	453

Ad valorem equivalents of base and bound tariffs:
Comparison to the ad valorem equivalent of unit market price support
Selected Commodities, Countries (%)

SKIM MILK POWDER[4]		1986-1988	1999-2000
US	AVE	166	72
	MPS	60	20
EC-12	AVE	146	84
	MPS	90	45
Canada	AVE	237	205
	MPS	102	77
Japan	AVE	311	229
	MPS	227	166
BEEF			
US	AVE	31	27
	MPS	7	1
EC-12	AVE	174	125
	MPS	90	81
Canada	AVE	38	27
	MPS	3	0
PIGMEAT			
EC-12	AVE	85	34
	MPS	40	10
Japan	AVE	130	119
	MPS	86	150

Notes and Sources: See pages 71 to 73.

Notes to Annex Table II.1

1. AVE refers to the ad valorem equivalent of the tariff which is bound in the schedule of the EC. INT+55%AVE refers to the ad valorem equivalent of a tariff applied in such a way that the duty-paid price will not exceed the intervention price increased by 55 percent of the intervention price. This rule, had it been applied to the 1986-1988 base period would have generated a level of protection significantly greater than the level of protection afforded by the bound tariff but will generally result in much lower levels of protection, compared to the bound tariff, during the implementation period of the Agreement.

2. Market price support has been measured at the wholesale level. Wholesale prices are much lower than producer prices because of government transfers. The wholesale price data used for the 1986-1988 period are as follows:

	1986	1987	1988
y/tonne	182 700	173 800	165 800

3. While the market price support component of the PSE calculations for sugar is presented at farm gate level, support prices are generally set at refinery level and the distribution of support between primary producers and processors is determined by formula. It has therefore been possible to derive the appropriate wholesale or ex-refinery prices from the PSE data bases and to recalculate MPS at or near the appropriate wholesale level which is comparable to the level at which the tariffs have been set.

4. The PSE calculations are done in respect of whole milk, support is estimated at the farm level and is not comparable with tariffs set at wholesale level for dairy products. Separate market price support calculations were undertaken to allow comparison with the new tariff levels. The external, world prices are New Zealand export prices reported to the GATT in the context of the International Dairy Agreement, and adjusted for transport costs to the relevant markets. Internal prices, which are either wholesale or support prices for the relevant dairy products, are derived from various domestic sources. The detailed definitions, sources and background data used in the calculations are presented in the supporting tables which follow:

Reference and domestic prices for dairy products

	Reference price	Domestic prices				
	New Zealand	United States	Canada	Japan	European Community	Australia
	US$ per T.	US$ per T.	C$ per T.	yen per T.	Ecu per T.	A$ per T.
SMP						
1986	817	1 777.8	2 945	541 200	1 875.2	1 543.0
1987	878	1 743.7	2 980	527 200	1 969.2	1 907.0
1988	1 667	1 765.3	3 007	521 200	1 979.3	2 672.0
Butter						
1986	1 060	3 185.2	4 976	1 021 957	3 374.6	2 331.0
1987	1 050	3 090.0	5 040	924 311	3 543.8	2 179.0
1988	1 258	2 919.9	5 095	897 571	3 562.0	2 116.0

Transportation costs

	Transportation costs from New-Zealand to:				
Units: US$/T	United States	Canada	Japan	European Community	Australia
SMP					
1986	77	77	63	79	100
1987	93	93	77	95	100
1988	95	95	77	95	96
Butter					
1986	181	181	145	152	127
1987	205	205	165	180	127
1988	510	510	165	180	127

5.　　The domestic price assumptions underlying these estimates are those which have been used in the development of the OECD's medium term projections and are reported in Tables 2 and 3 of the Agricultural Outlook 1995-2000 (OECD 1995b). The world price projections underlying the estimates are also drawn from the various tables in the Agricultural Outlook and have been reproduced in Table 9 of this document. For beef and pigmeat, as the medium term outlook does not generate a medium term projection the trend in the United States domestic price has been used as a proxy, except in the case of EC beef markets. The projected trend in the Argentinian unit export value for beef has been used as a proxy for the external reference price for EC-12 (Source: World Bank) and the projected evolution of the world price for sugar has also been provided by the World Bank. Those price projections [expressed as an index (base 1994 = 100)], that are not derived from the OECD's medium term outlook exercise are as follows:

World Bank price projections 1995-2000

	1994	1995	1996	1997	1998	1999	2000
Refined sugar	100	109	98	97	106	103	103
Beef (Argentina)	100	99	97	102	104	103	104

Some Additional Details on Aspects of the Methodology.

The methodology employed to calculate the elements of Table II.1 has been summarised in the first paragraph of this annex and in the notes to Table II.1. Some additional information on methodology is presented here.

The abbreviations and terminology used in Table II.1 are as follows:

i)　　AVE refers to the ad valorem equivalent of the tariffs bound in country schedules. Where the tariff is expressed as an ad valorem rate, it is simply reproduced in the Table. Where the bound rate is a specific duty or a combination of an ad valorem and a specific rate, the ad valorem equivalent has been calculated using as the denominator the external reference price which is used in the calculation of market price support. Some countries have specified a minimum specific tariff to be applied in cases where the ad valorem tariff would yield a specific tariff lower than that minimum. Where this is the case the higher tariff, i.e. the tariff which would actually apply, is reported in the Table.

ii)　　MPS refers to the unit market price support expressed as an ad valorem equivalent tariff where the denominator is again the external reference price which is used in the calculation of the market price support. Where appropriate and feasible the calculation of the unit market price support has been adjusted in order to be comparable to tariffs which were set by reference to differences between wholesale and world prices. This has been done in the case of sugar, butter, skim milk powder (all countries shown in the table) and wheat (in Japan, where wholesale prices are actually lower than producer prices). Where it has not been possible to identify wholesale prices, support prices defined at wholesale or ex-factory level have been used. For the products listed above, therefore, the ad valorem equivalents of the tariffs and the ad valorem equivalents of the market price support estimates are estimated at the same point in the agro-food chain. For the other commodities (wheat other than for Japan, beef and pigmeat for all countries shown) the market price support estimate has been made at producer price level. This implies that the difference between the AVE and the MPS estimates has been overestimated to the extent that the market price support calculation does not reflect the producer to wholesale price margin.

Sources for the Skim milk powder and butter calculations in Table II.1

Skim milk powder	Producer price	Reference price
United States	1986-1988: USDA 1999-2000: Wholesale price assumption, fob plant, central states, extra grade.	1986-1988: GATT IDA price +transport costs NZ-US 1999-2000: Extrapolation using world price projection, OECD Agricultural Outlook 1995-2000, table 17.
Japan	1986-1988: Stabilisation indicative price. 1999-2000: Stabilisation price assumption from OECD Agricultural Outlook 1995-2000, table 3.	1986-1988: GATT IDA price +transport costs NZ-Japan. 1999-2000: Extrapolation using world price projection, OECD Agricultural Outlook 1995-2000, table 17.
Canada	1986-1988: Support price, OECD Agricultural Outlook 1995-2000, table 3. 1999-2000: Average wholesale price assumption , OECD Agricultural Outlook 1995-2000, table 21 .	1986-1988: GATT IDA price +transport costs NZ-US 1999-2000: Extrapolation using world price projection, OECD Agricultural Outlook 1995-2000, table 17.
European Community	1986-1988: Intervention price SMP spray (in Green Ecu*switchover), CAP Monitor, Agra-Europe. 1999-2000: Support price assumption , OECD Agricultural Outlook 1995-2000, table 3.	1986-1988: GATT IDA price +transport costs NZ-Europe. 1999-2000: Extrapolation using world price projection, OECD Agricultural Outlook 1995-2000, table 17.
Australia	1986-1988: Producer returns on exports + unit export subsidy. 1999-2000: Average domestic price, OECD Agricultural Outlook 1995-2000, table 21.	1986-1988: GATT IDA price +transport costs NZ-Australia. 1999-2000: Extrapolation using world price projection, OECD Agricultural Outlook 1995-2000, table 17.

Butter	Producer price	Reference price
United States	1986-1988: Wholesale prices for butter grade A, Chicago. 1999-2000: Wholesale price assumption for butter grade A, Chicago, OECD Agricultural Outlook, 1995-2000., table 19.	1986-1988: GATT IDA price +transport costs NZ-US. 1999-2000: Extrapolation using world price projection, OECD Agricultural Outlook 1995-2000, table 17.
Japan	1986-1988: Stabilisation indicative price. 1999-2000: Stabilisation (support) price assumption, OECD Agricultural Outlook, 1995-2000, table 3.	1986-1988: GATT IDA price +transport costs NZ-Japan. 1999-2000: Extrapolation using world price projection, OECD Agricultural Outlook 1995-2000, table 17.
Canada	1986-1988: Wholesale support price. 1999-2000: Wholesale support price assumption, OECD Agricultural Outlook, 1995-2000, table 19.	1986-1988: GATT IDA price +transport costs NZ-US 1999-2000: Extrapolation using world price projection, OECD Agricultural Outlook 1995-2000, table 17.
European Community	1986-1988: Intervention price (in Green Ecu*switchover), CAP Monitor, Agra-Europe. 1999-2000: Support price assumption , OECD Agricultural Outlook 1995-2000, table 3.	1986-1988: GATT IDA price +transport costs NZ-Europe 1999-2000: Extrapolation using world price projection, OECD Agricultural Outlook 1995-2000, table 17.
Australia	1986-1988: Producer return on exports + unit export subsidy. 1999-2000: Market price assumption (Export price + % MPS for manufactured grade milk) , OECD Agricultural Outlook 1995-2000 table 19 + Aglink model.	1986-1988: GATT IDA price +transport costs NZ-Australia 1999-2000: Extrapolation using world price projection, OECD Agricultural Outlook 1995-2000, table 17.

Annex III

DETAILED COUNTRY TABLES

Table III.1. Uruguay Round Agricultural Negotiations: US Country Schedule. Tariffs: reduction commitments

Code		Product	Units	Base rate of duty 1	Bound rate of duty 2	Percentage reduction	Special safeguard	Commitments					
								1995	1996	1997	1998	1999	2000
10019020	1	**Wheat** Common wheat	$/t	7.7	3.5	55%		7	6	6	5	4	4
10011000	2	Durum wheat	$/t	7.7	6.5	16%		8	7	7	7	7	7
10059040	3	**Coarse grains** Maize	$/t	9.8	2.5	74%		9	7	6	5	4	3
10030040	4	Barley	$/t	3.4	1.5	56%		3	3	2	2	2	2
10040000	5	Oats	$/t	0	0			0	0	0	0	0	0
10070000	6	Sorghum	$/t	8.8	2.2	75%		8	7	6	4	3	2
10062040	7	Rice	$/t	33	21	36%		31	29	27	25	23	21
12010000	8	**Oilseeds** Soyabeans		0	0			0	0	0	0	0	0
12050000	9	Rapeseed	$/t	9	5.8	36%		8	8	7	7	6	6
12060000	10	Sunflower		0	0			0	0	0	0	0	0
17011150	11	**Sugar** Raw (cane) sugar	$/t	399	339	15%	yes	389	379	369	359	349	339
17011250	12	Raw (beet) sugar	$/t	421	357	15%	yes	410	399	389	378	368	357
17019950	13	Refined sugar	$/t	421	357	15%	yes	410	399	389	378	368	357
04012040	14	**Milk** Liquid milk (human cons.)	$/L	0.017	0.015	12%							
04012040	15	Liquid milk (human cons.)	$/t	175	154	15%		172	168	165	161	158	154
04022190	16	Skim milk powder	$/t	1 831	1 556	15%	yes	1 785	1 739	1 694	1 648	1 602	1 556
04050040	17	Butter	$/t	1 813	1 541	15%	yes	1 768	1 722	1 677	1 632	1 586	1 541
04061068	18	Cheese (Emmental)	$/t	1 631	1 386	15%	yes	1 590	1 549	1 509	1 468	1 427	1 386
04061028	19	Cheese (Cheddar)	$/t	1 443	1 227	15%	yes	1 407	1 371	1 335	1 299	1 263	1 227
01029040	20	**Beef and veal** Live animals	$/t	22	10	55%	yes	20	18	16	14	12	10
02011050	21	Beef meat	%	31%	26.4%	15%		30.3	29.5	28.7	28.0	27.3	26.4
02031100	22	**Pigmeat**	$/t	0	0			0	0	0	0	0	0
02071040	23	**Poultrymeat**	$/t	110	88	20%		106	103	99	95	92	88
02042100	24	**Sheepmeat** Sheepmeat	$/t	33	28	15%	yes	32	31	31	30	29	28
02041000	25	Lamb	$/t	11	7	36%		10	10	9	8	8	7
51011960	26	**Wool**	$/t	220	187	15%		215	209	204	198	193	187
04070000	27	**Eggs** Eggs	$/DOZ	0.035	0.028	20%							
		Eggs	$/t	49	40	20%		48	46	44	43	41	40

1. Average of 1986-88 .

2. Year of implementation of bound rate of duty = 2000

Table III.2. Uruguay Round Agricultural Negotiations: EC Country Schedule. Tariffs : reduction commitments

Code		Product	Base rate of duty 1 (Ecu/T or %)	Bound rate of duty 2 (Ecu/T or %)	Percentage reduction	Special safeguard	Commitments (Ecu/T or %) 1995	1996	1997	1998	1999	2000
		Wheat										
10019095	1	Common wheat	149	95	36%	yes	140	131	122	113	104	95
10011050	2	Durum wheat	231	148	36%	yes	217	203	190	176	162	148
		Coarse grains										
10059000	3	Maize	147	94	36%	yes	138	129	121	112	103	94
10030050	4	Barley	145	93	36%	yes	136	128	119	110	102	93
10040050	5	Oats	139	89	36%	yes	131	122	114	106	97	89
10061060	6	Rice	330	211	36%	yes	310	290	271	251	231	211
		Oilseeds										
12010090	7	Soyabeans	—	—								
12050090	8	Rapeseed	—	—								
12060090	9	Sunflower	—	—								
		Sugar										
17011110	10	Raw (cane) sugar	424	339	20%	yes	410	396	382	367	353	339
17019950	11	Refined sugar	524	419	20%	yes	507	489	472	454	437	419
		Milk										
04012091	12	Liquid milk (human cons.)	354	227	36%	yes	333	312	291	269	248	227
04021019	13	Skim milk powder	1 485	1 188	20%	yes	1 436	1 386	1 337	1 287	1 238	1 188
04050010	14	Butter	2 962	1 896	36%	yes	2 784	2 607	2 429	2 251	2 074	1 896
04069014	15	Cheese (Emmental)	274	175	36%	yes	257	241	225	208	192	175
04069021	16	Cheese (Cheddar)	2 611	1 671	36%	yes	2 454	2 298	2 141	1 984	1 828	1 671
		Beef and veal[3]										
01029020	17	Live animals[3]	16.0% / 1454	10.2% / 931	36%	yes	15.0% / 1367	14.1% / 1280	13.1% / 1193	12.1% / 1105	11.2% / 1018	10.2% / 931
02021000	18	Beefmeat	20.0% / 2763	12.8% / 1768	36%	yes	18.8% / 2522	17.6% / 2371	16.4% / 2221	15.2% / 2070	14.0% / 1919	12.8% / 1768
		Pigmeat										
02032110	19	Pigmeat	838	536	36%	yes	788	737	687	637	586	536
		Poultrymeat										
02071011	20	Poultrymeat	410	262	36%	yes	385	361	336	311	287	262
		Sheepmeat										
02042100	21	Lamb	20.0% / 2 677	12.8% / 1 713	36%	yes	18.8% / 2516	17.6% / 2 356	16.4% / 2 195	15.2% / 2 034	14.0% / 1 874	12.8% / 1 713
51012100	22	Wool	free	free		yes						
04070030	23	Eggs	475	304	36%	yes	447	418	390	361	333	304

1. Average of 1986-88.
2. Year of implementation of bound rate of duty = 2000.
3. For products in lines 17,18 and 21 tariffs are made of two combined elements: an ad-valorem plus a specific rate.

Table III.3. Uruguay Round Agricultural Negotiations: Japan Country Schedule. Tariffs: reduction commitments

Code		Product	Base rate of duty 1	Bound rate of duty 2	Percentage reduction	Special safeguard	Commitments 1995	1996	1997	1998	1999	2000
			(Yen/T or %)	(Yen/T or %)			(Yen/T or %)					
		Wheat										
10019000	1	Common wheat	65 000	55 000	15%	yes	63 333	61 667	60 000	58 333	56 667	55 000
10011000	2	Durum wheat	65 000	55 000	15%	yes	63 333	61 667	60 000	58 333	56 667	55 000
		Coarse Grains										
10059000	3	Maize for feed	0	0			0	0	0	0	0	0
10059000	4	Maize, other	15 000	12 000	20%	yes	12 000	12 000	12 000	12 000	12 000	12 000
10030000	5	Barley	46 000	39 000	15%		44 833	43 667	42 500	41 333	40 167	39 000
10040000	6	Oats	10.0%	8.5%	15%		9.8%	9.5%	9.3%	9.0%	8.8%	8.5%
10061000	7	Rice	–	–	–		–			–	–	–
		Oilseeds										
12010000	8	Soyabeans	0	0			0	0	0	0	0	0
12050000	9	Rapeseed	0	0			0	0	0	0	0	0
12060000	10	Sunflower	0	0			0	0	0	0	0	0
		Sugar										
17011100	11	Raw (cane) sugar	84 500	71 800	15%		82 383	80 267	78 150	76033	73 917	71 800
17019900	12	Refined sugar	121 300	103 100	15%		118 267	115 233	112 200	109 167	106 133	103 100
		Milk & Dairy Products										
04012000	13	Liquid milk	25.0% / 134 000	21.3% / 114 000	15% / 15%	yes	24.4% / 130 667	23.8% / 127 333	23.2% / 124 000	22.5% / 120 667	21.9% / 117 333	21.3% / 114 000
04021000	14	Skim milk powder	25.0% / 466 000	21.3% / 396 000	15% / 15%	yes	24.4% / 454 333	23.8% / 442 667	23.2% / 431 000	22.5% / 419 333	21.9% / 407 667	21.3% / 39 6000
04050000	15	Butter	35.0% / 1 159 000	29.8% / 985 000	15% / 15%	yes	34.1% / 1 130 000	33.3% / 1 101 000	32.4% / 1 072 000	31.5% / 1 043 000	30.7% / 1 014 000	29.8% / 98 5000
04061000	16	Cheese (Fresh)	35.0%	29.8%	15%		34.1%	33.3%	32.4%	31.5%	30.7%	29.8%
04063000	17	Cheese (Processed)	79.7%	40.0%	50%		40.0%	40.0%	40.0%	40.0%	40.0%	40.0%
		Beef and Veal										
010290	18	Live animals	45 000	38 250	15%		43875	42 750	41625	40500	39 375	38 250
020110	19	Beefmeat	93.0%	50.0%	46%		48.1%	46.2%	44.3%	42.3%	40.4%	38.5%
		Pigmeat										
	20	Gate Price	553 000	489 000	12%		542 000	532 000	521 000	511 000	500 000	489 000
020311	21	Pigmeat (specific)	425 000	361 000	15%	yes	414 333	403 667	393 000	382 333	371 667	361 000
020311	22	Pigmeat (ad val.)	5.0%	4.3%	15%	yes	4.9%	4.8%	4.6%	4.5%	4.4%	4.3%
		Poultrymeat										
020710	23	Poultrymeat	14.0%	11.9%	15%		13.7%	13.3%	13.0%	12.6%	12.3%	11.9
		Sheepmeat										
020421	24	Lamb	0	0			0	0	0	0	0	0
510121	25	Wool	0	0			0	0	0	0	0	0
040700	26	Eggs	20.0%	17.0%	15%		19.5%	19.0%	18.5%	18.0%	17.5%	17.0%

1. Average of 1986-88 .
2. Year of implementation of bound rate of duty = 2000.
3. For products in lines 13, 14 and 15, tariffs are made of two combined elements: an ad-valorem plus a specific rate.

Table III.4. **Uruguay Round Agricultural Negotiations: Canada Country Schedule. Tariffs: reduction commitments**

Code		Product	Base rate of duty 1 Specific rate (C$/T)	Base rate of duty 1 ad valorem (%)	Bound rate of duty 2 Specific rate (C$/T)	Bound rate of duty 2 ad valorem (%)	Percentage reduction	Special safeguard	1995	1996	1997	1998	1999	2000
		Wheat												
10019020	1	Common wheat		90.0%		76.5%	15%	yes	87.8%	85.5%	83.3%	81.0%	78.8%	76.5%
10011020	2	Durum wheat		57.7%		49.0%	15%	yes	56.3%	54.8%	53.4%	51.9%	50.5%	49.0%
		Coarse grains												
10051010	3	Maize	1.97		1.26		36%		1.85	1.73	1.62	1.50	1.38	1.26
10030012	4	Barley		111.4%		94.7%	15%	yes	108.6%	105.8%	103.1%	100.3%	97.5%	94.7%
10040020	5	Oats	18.12		0		100%		15	12	9	6	3	0%
10062000	6	Rice	free		free				0%	0%	0%	0%	0%	0%
		Oilseeds												
12010000	7	Soyabeans	free		free		15%		0%	0%	0%	0%	0%	0%
12050090	8	Rapeseed	free		free		15%		0%	0%	0%	0%	0%	0%
12060090	9	Sunflower	free		free		15%		0%	0%	0%	0%	0%	0%
		Sugar												
17011150	10	Raw (cane) sugar	32.54		27.66		15%		31.73	30.91	30.10	29.29	28.47	27.66
17019900	11	Refined sugar	41.67		35.42		15%		40.63	39.59	38.55	37.50	36.46	35.42
		Milk												
04012020	12	Liquid milk (hum.cons.)		283.8%		241.3%	15%	yes	276.3%	269.3%	262.3%	255.3%	248.3%	241.3%
		min C$/hl	40.6		34.5		15%	yes	39.6	38.6	37.6	36.5	35.5	34.5
04021020	13	SMP		237.2%		201.6%	15%	yes	231.3%	225.3%	219.4%	213.5%	207.5%	201.6%
		min	2 360		2 006		15%		2301	2242	2183	2124	2065	2006
04050012	14	Butter		351.4%		298.7%	15%	yes	342.6%	333.8%	325.1%	316.3%	307.5%	298.7%
		min	4 708		4 001		15%		4590	4472	4355	4237	4119	4 001
04069012	15	Cheese		289.0%		245.6%	15%	yes	281.8%	274.5%	267.3%	260.1%	252.8%	245.6%
		(Cheddar) min	4 149		3 528		15%		4046	3942	3839	3735	3632	3 528
		Beef and veal												
01029090	16	Live animals[3]	22		11		50%		20	18	17	15	13	11
02011020	17	Beefmeat[4]		37.9%		26.5%	30%	yes	36.0%	34.1%	32.2%	30.3%	28.4%	26.5%
		Pigmeat												
02031100	18	Pigmeat		Free		Free	0.0%		0.0%	0.0%	0.0%	0.0%	0.0%	0.0%
		Poultrymeat												
02071019	19	Poultrymeat		280.4%		238.3%	15%	yes	273.4%	266.4%	259.4%	252.3%	245.3%	238.3%
		min	1960		1666		15%		1911	1862	1813	1764	1715	1 666
02071024	20	Turkey		182.0%		154.7%	15%	yes	177.3%	172.7%	168.0%	163.3%	158.7%	154.0%
		min	2295		1951		15%		2238	2180	2123	2066	2008	1 951
		Sheepmeat												
02042100	21	Lamb	66.1		42.3		36%		621	582	542	502	463	423
51012100	22	Wool	Free		Free				0%	0%	0%	0%	0%	0%
		Eggs												
04070012	23	Eggs		280.4%		238.3%	15%		273.4%	266.4%	259.4%	252.3%	245.3%	238.3%
		min	5 037.7		4 280.6		15%		4 911.5	4 785.3	4 659.2	4 533.0	4 406.8	4 280.6
04070019	24	Eggs		192.3%		163.5%	15%		187.5%	182.7%	177.9%	173.1%	168.3%	163.5%
		min	1 381.8		1 174.5		15%		1347.3	1312.7	1278.2	1243.6	1209.1	1 174.5

1. Average of 1986-88. 2. Year of implementation of bound rate of duty = 2000   3. All other categories of live animals enter free
4. The tariff will be reduced to match the level of the US tariff upon implementation.

Table III.5. Uruguay Round Agricultural Negotiations: New Zealand Country Schedule. Tariffs: reduction commitments

Code		Product	Base rate of duty 1 (NZ$/T or %)	Bound rate of duty 2 (NZ$/T or %)	Percentage reduction	Special safeguard	Commitments (NZ$/T or %)					
							1995	1996	1997	1998	1999	2000
		Wheat										
10019000	1	Common wheat	0	0	n.a.		0	0	0	0	0	0
10011000	2	Durum wheat	0	0	n.a.		0	0	0	0	0	0
		Coarse grains										
10059000	3	Maize	0	0	n.a.		0	0	0	0	0	0
10030000	4	Barley	10.0%	5.0%	50%		9.2%	8.3%	7.5%	6.7%	5.8%	5.0%
10040000	5	Oats	10.0%	7.5%	25%		9.6%	9.2%	8.8%	8.3%	7.9%	7.5%
10061000	6	Rice	0	0	n.a.		0	0	0	0	0	0
		Oilseeds										
12010000	7	Soyabeans	0	0	n.a.		0	0	0	0	0	0
12050000	8	Rapeseed	0	0	n.a.		0	0	0	0	0	0
12060000	9	Sunflower	0	0	n.a.		0	0	0	0	0	0
		Sugar										
17011100	10	Raw (cane) sugar	0.915	0.000			0.763	0.610	0.458	0.305	0.153	0.000
17019900	11	Refined sugar	0	0			0	0	0	0	0	0
		Milk										
04012001	12	Liquid milk (human cons.)	10.0%	7.5%	25%		9.6%	9.2%	8.8%	8.3%	7.9%	7.5%
04021000	13	Skim milk powder	20.0%	12.8%	36%		18.8%	17.6%	16.4%	15.2%	14.0%	12.8%
04050000	14	Butter	10.0%	6.4%	36%		9.4%	8.8%	8.2%	7.6%	7.0%	6.4%
04069000	15	Cheese	20.0%	12.8%	36%		18.8%	17.6%	16.4%	15.2%	14.0%	12.8%
		Beef and veal										
01029000	17	Live animals	0	0	n.a.		0	0	0	0	0	0
02011000	18	Beefmeat	0	0	n.a.		0	0	0	0	0	0
		Pigmeat										
02031100	19	Pigmeat	20.0%	8.5%	58%		18.1%	16.2%	14.3%	12.3%	10.4%	8.5%
		Poultrymeat										
02071000	20	Poultrymeat	28.5%	18.2%	36%		26.8%	25.1%	23.4%	21.6%	19.9%	18.2%
		Sheepmeat										
02041000	21	Lamb	0	0	n.a.		0	0	0	0	0	0
51011100	22	Wool	0	0	n.a.		0	0	0	0	0	0
04070000	23	Eggs	0	0	n.a.		0	0	0	0	0	0

1. Average of 1986-88.

2. Year of implementation of bound rate of duty = 2000.

Table III.6. **Uruguay Round Agricultural Negotiations: Australia Country Schedule. Tariffs: reduction commitments**

Code		Product	Base rate of duty 1 (A$/T or %)	Bound rate of duty 2 (A$/T or %)	Percentage reduction	Special safeguard	Commitments (A$/T or %)					
							1995	1996	1997	1998	1999	2000
		Wheat										
10019000	1	Common wheat	0	0	—		0	0	0	0	0	0
10011000	2	Durum wheat	0	0	—		0	0	0	0	0	0
		Coarse grains										
10059000	3	Maize	2%	1%	50%		1.8%	1.7%	1.5%	1.3%	1.2%	1.0%
10030000	4	Barley	0	0	—		0	0	0	0	0	0
10040000	5	Oats	0	0	—		0	0	0	0	0	0
10061000	6	Rice	2%	1%	50%		1.8%	1.7%	1.5%	1.3%	1.2%	1.0%
		Oilseeds										
12010000	7	Soyabeans	2%	1%	50%		1.8%	1.7%	1.5%	1.3%	1.2%	1.0%
12050090	8	Rapeseed	2%	1%	50%		1.8%	1.7%	1.5%	1.3%	1.2%	1.0%
12060090	9	Sunflower	2%	1%	50%		1.8%	1.7%	1.5%	1.3%	1.2%	1.0%
		Sugar										
170111	10	Raw (cane) sugar	140	70	50%		128	117	105	93	82	70
17019990	11	Refined sugar	140	70	50%		128	117	105	93	82	70
		Milk										
04012091	12	Liquid milk (cons.)	0	0	—		0	0	0	0	0	0
04021019	13	Skim milk powder	50	1%	nc.		N.C.	N.C.	N.C.	N.C.	N.C.	1%
04030000	14	Yogurt, etc.	50	1%	nc.		N.C.	N.C.	N.C.	N.C.	N.C.	1%
04050010	15	Butter	100	1%	nc.		N.C.	N.C.	N.C.	N.C.	N.C.	1%
04069000	16	Cheese	1 440	1 220	15%	yes	1 403	1 367	1 330	1 293	1 257	1 220
		Beef and veal										
01029000	17	Live animals	2%	1%	50%		1.8%	1.7%	1.5%	1.3%	1.2%	1%
02021000	18	Beef	0	0	—		0	0	0	0	0	0
		Pigmeat										
02032110	19	Pigmeat	0	0	—		0	0	0	0	0	0
		Poultrymeat										
02071011	20	Poultrymeat	0	0	—		0	0	0	0	0	0
		Sheepmeat										
02042100	21	Lamb	0	0	—		0	0	0	0	0	0
51012100	22	Wool	2%	1%	50%		1.8%	1.7%	1.5%	1.3%	1.2%	1.0%
04070030	23	Eggs	120	0	100%		100	80	60	40	20	0

1. Average of 1986-88.

2. Year of implementation of bound rate of duty = 2000.

N.C. = Not Computable

81

Table III.7. Uruguay Round Agricultural Negotiations: Switzerland Country Schedule. Tariffs: reduction commitments

Code	Product		Units	Base rate of duty 1	Bound rate of duty 2	Percentage reduction	Special safeguard	Commitments (SF/T)					
								1995	1996	1997	1998	1999	2000
	Wheat												
10019010	Common wheat	1	SF/t	890	760	15%	yes	868	847	825	803	782	760
10011010	Durum wheat	2	SF/t	870	740	15%	yes	848	827	805	783	762	740
	Coarse grains												
10059000	Maize	3	SF/t	550	350	36%	yes	517	483	450	417	383	350
10030000	Barley	4	SF/t	580	370	36%	yes	545	510	475	440	405	370
10040000	Oats	5	SF/t	500	350	30%	yes	475	450	425	400	375	350
10061000	Rice	6	SF/t	6	0	100%	yes	5	4	3	2	1	0
	Oilseeds												
12010000	Soyabeans	7	SF/t	610	390	36%	yes	573	537	500	463	427	390
12050000	Rapeseed	8	SF/t	630	440	30%	yes	598	567	535	503	472	440
12060000	Sunflower	9	SF/t	620	430	31%	yes	588	557	525	493	462	430
	Sugar												
17011200	Raw (beet) sugar	10	SF/t	720	610	15%	yes	702	683	665	647	628	610
17019900	Refined sugar	11	SF/t	720	610	15%	yes	702	683	665	647	628	610
	Milk												
04012000	Liquid milk (human cons.)	12	SF/t	890	760	15%	yes	868	847	825	803	782	760
04021000	Skim milk powder	13	SF/t	3 800	3 230	15%	yes	3 705	3 610	3 515	3 420	3325	3 230
04050010	Butter	14	SF/t	19 320	16 420	15%	yes	18 837	18 353	17 870	17 387	16 903	16 420
04069029	Cheese (Emmental)	15	SF/t	480	408	15%	yes	468	456	444	432	420	408
	Beef and veal												
01029010	Live animals[3]	16	SF/t	75 000	63 750	15%	yes	73 125	71250	69 375	67 500	65 625	63 750
02011000	Beef meat	17	SF/t	8 920	7 580	15%	yes	8 697	8 473	8 250	8 027	7 803	7 580
	Pigmeat												
02031100	Pigmeat	18	SF/t	4 080	3 470	15%	yes	3 978	3 877	3 775	3 673	3 572	3 470
02071000	Poultrymeat Poultrymeat	19	SF/t	3 670	3 120	15%	yes	3 578	3 487	3 395	3 303	3 212	3 120
	Sheepmeat												
02042100	Sheepmeat	20	SF/t	9 940	8 450	15%	yes	9 692	9 443	9 195	8 947	8 698	8 450
02041000	Lamb	21	SF/t	9 860	8 380	15%	yes	96 13	9 367	9 120	8 873	8 27	8 380
51011100	Wool	22	SF/t	1.5	0	100%	yes	1	1	1	1	0	0
	Eggs												
04070000	Eggs	23	SF/t	4 370	3 710	15%	yes	4 260	4 150	4 040	3 930	3 820	3 710

1. Average of 1986-88
2. Year of implementation of bound rate of duty = 2000.
3. Conversion coefficient for live animals: divide by 0.2.

Table III.8. Uruguay Round Agricultural Negotiations: Norway Country Schedule. Tariffs: reduction commitments

Code	Product	Base rate of duty 1 (NKr/T or %)	Bound rate of duty 2 (NKr/T or %)	Percentage reduction	Special safeguard	Commitments (NKr/T or %) 1995	1996	1997	1998	1999	2000
	Wheat										
10011000 (1)	Durum wheat	3 040	2 130	30%	yes	2 890	2 740	2 590	2 440	2290	2 130
	or	495	347	30%		470	445	420	395	370	347
	Coarse Grains										
10020000 (2)	Rye	3 040	2 130	30%	yes	2 890	2 740	2 590	2 440	2290	2 130
	or	495	347	30%		470	445	420	395	370	347
10030000 (3)	Barley	2 490	1 740	30%	yes	2 370	2 250	2 130	2 010	1 890	1 740
	or	454	318	30%		431	408	385	362	339	318
10040000 (4)	Oats	2 030	1 520	30%	yes	1 950	1 870	1 790	1 710	1 630	1 520
	or	310	233	25%		297	284	271	258	245	233
10050000 (5)	Maize	2 540	1 780	25%	yes	2 410	2 280	2 150	2 020	1 890	1 780
	or	490	343	30%		466	442	418	394	370	343
	Rice										
10061000 (6)	Rice (for feed)	2 490	1 740	30%	yes	2 370	2 250	2 130	2 010	1 890	1 740
	or	454	318	30%		431	408	385	362	339	318
	Oilseeds										
12010000 (7)	Soyabeans	3 830	2 680	30%	yes	3 640	3 450	3 260	3 070	2 880	2 680
	or	296	207	30%		281	266	251	236	221	207
12050000 (8)	Rapeseeds	4 870	3 410	30%	yes	4 630	4 390	4 150	3 910	3 670	3 410
	or	383	268	30%		364	345	326	307	288	268
12060000 (9)	Sunflowerseeds	4 870	3 410	30%	yes	4 630	4 390	4 150	3 910	3 670	3 410
	or	383	268	30%		364	345	326	307	288	268
	Sugar										
17011100 (10)	Raw (cane) sugar	100	30	70%		88	76	64	52	40	30
	or	100	30	70%		88	76	64	52	40	30
17019909 (11)	Refined sugar	100	30	70%		88	76	64	52	40	30
	or	100	30	70%		88	76	64	52	40	30
	Milk & Dairy Products										
04012000 (12)	Liquid milk	5 250	4 460	15%	yes	5 120	4 990	4 860	4730	4 600	4 460
	or	457	388	15%		446	435	424	413	402	388
04021000 (13)	Skimmed milk powder	26 910	22 870	15%	yes	26 240	25 570	24 900	24 230	23 560	22 870
	or	461	392	15%		450	439	428	417	406	392
04050000 (14)	Butter	29 640	25 190	15%	yes	28 900	28 160	27 420	26 680	25 940	25 190
	or	403	343	15%		393	383	373	363	353	343
04061000 (15)	Cheese (Fresh)	29 030	24 680	15%	yes	28 310	27 590	26 870	26 150	25 430	24 680
	or	275	233	15%		268	261	254	247	240	233
04063000 (16)	Cheese (Processed)	32 980	28 040	15%	yes	32 160	31 340	30 520	29 700	28 880	28 040
	or	312	265	15%		304	296	288	280	272	265
	Beef and Veal										
01029000 (17)	Live animals	44 250	37 610	15%	yes	43 140	42 030	40 920	39 810	38 700	37 610
	or	405	344	15%		395	385	375	365	355	344
02011000 (18)	Beefmeat	37 970	32 280	15%	yes	37 020	36 070	35 120	34 170	33 220	32 280
	or	405	344	15%		395	385	375	365	355	344
	Pigmeat										
02031100 (19)	Pigmeat	28 990	24 640	15%	yes	28 270	27 550	26 830	26 110	25 390	24 640
	or	428	363	15%		417	406	395	384	373	363
	Poultrymeat										
02071000 (20)	Poultrymeat	56 940	48 400	15%	yes	55 520	54 100	52 680	51 260	49 840	48 400
	or	500	425	15%		488	476	464	452	440	425
	Sheepmeat										
02042100 (21)	Mutton	28 410	24 150	15%	yes	27 700	26 990	26 280	25 570	24 860	24 150
	or	505	429	15%		492	479	466	453	440	429
	Wool										
51012100 (22)	Shorn wool	0	0			0	0	0	0	0	0
	or	0	0								
	Eggs										
04070010 (23)	Hen's egg	15 740	12 590	20%	yes	15 220	14 700	14 180	13 660	13 140	12 590
	or	340	272	20%		329	318	307	296	285	272

1. Average of 1986-88. 2. Year of implementation of bound rate of dute = 2000. 3. Norway has set both a specific and ad valorem rate for most products. The highest will apply.

Table III.9. Uruguay Round Agricultural Negotiations: Iceland Country Schedule. Tariffs: reduction commitments

Code		Product	Base rate of duty 1	Bound rate of duty 2	Percentage reduction	Special safeguard	Commitments					
							1995	1996	1997	1998	1999	2000
		Wheat										
10019000	1	Common wheat	0	0	n.a.		0%	0%	0%	0%	0%	0%
		– except for feed purpose	350%	175%	50%	yes	321%	292%	263%	233%	204%	175%
10011000	2	Durum wheat	0	0	n.a.		0%	0%	0%	0%	0%	0%
		– except for feed purpose	350%	175%	50%	yes	321%	292%	263%	233%	204%	175%
		Coarse grains										
10059000	3	Maize	0	0	n.a.		0%	0%	0%	0%	0%	0%
		– except for feed purpose	350%	175%	50%	yes	321%	292%	263%	233%	204%	175%
10030000	4	Barley	0	0	n.a.		0%	0%	0%	0%	0%	0%
		– except for feed purpose	350%	175%	50%	yes	321%	292%	263%	233%	204%	175%
10040000	5	Oats	0	0	n.a.		0%	0%	0%	0%	0%	0%
		– except for feed purpose	350%	175%	50%	yes	321%	292%	263%	233%	204%	175%
10061009	6	Rice	0	0	n.a.		0%	0%	0%	0%	0%	0%
		– except for feed purpose	350%	175%	50%	yes	321%	292%	263%	233%	204%	175%
		Oilseeds										
12010000	7	Soyabeans	0	0	n.a.		0%	0%	0%	0%	0%	0%
		– except for feed purpose	350%	175%	50%	yes	321%	292%	263%	233%	204%	175%
12050000	8	Rapeseed	0	0	n.a.		0%	0%	0%	0%	0%	0%
		– except for feed purpose	350%	175%	50%	yes	321%	292%	263%	233%	204%	175%
12060000	9	Sunflower	0	0	n.a.		0%	0%	0%	0%	0%	0%
		– except for feed purpose	350%	175%	50%	yes	321%	292%	263%	233%	204%	175%
		Sugar										
17011100	10	Raw (cane) sugar	0	0	n.a.		0%	0%	0%	0%	0%	0%
		– except for feed purpose	350%	175%	50%	yes	321%	292%	263%	233%	204%	175%
17019909	11	Refine sugar	0	0	n.a.		0%	0%	0%	0%	0%	0%
		– except for feed purpose	350%	175%	50%	yes	321%	292%	263%	233%	204%	175%
		Milk										
04012000	12	Liquid milk (human cons.)	586%	498%	15%	yes	571%	557%	542%	527%	513%	498%
04021000	13	Skim milk powder	527%	448%	15%	yes	514%	501%	488%	474%	461%	448%
04050000	14	Butter	674%	573%	15%	yes	657%	640%	624%	607%	590%	573%
04069000	15	Cheese	578%	491%	15%	yes	564%	549%	535%	520%	506%	491%
		Beef and veal										
01029000	16	Live animals	358%	229%	36%	yes	337%	315%	294%	272%	251%	229%
							0%	0%	0%	0%	0%	0%
02011000	17	Beefmeat	358%	304%	15%	yes	349%	340%	331%	322%	313%	304%
							0%	0%	0%	0%	0%	0%
		Pigmeat										
02031100	18	Pigmeat	538%	457%	15%	yes	525%	511%	498%	484%	471%	457%
		Poultrymeat										
02072100	19	Poultrymeat	467%	397%	15%	yes	455%	444%	432%	420%	409%	397%
		Sheepmeat										
02041000	20	Lamb	397%	337%	15%	yes	387%	377%	367%	357%	347%	337%
51011100	21	Wool	0	0	n.a.		0%	0%	0%	0%	0%	0%
04070000	22	Eggs	478%	406%	15%	yes	466%	454%	442%	430%	418%	406%

1. Average of 1986-88. 2. Year of implementation of bound rate of duty = 2000.

Table III.10. Uruguay Round Agricultural Negotiations: Mexico Country Schedule. Tariffs: reduction commitments

Code		Product	Base rate of duty 1 (US$/T or %)	Bound rate of duty 2 (US$/T or %)	Percentage reduction	Special safeguard	Commitments (US$/T or %)									
							1995	1996	1997	1998	1999	2000	2001	2002	2003	2004
		Wheat														
10019099	1	Common wheat	100 / 74%	or 90 / 67%	10% / 9%	yes	99 / 73%	98 / 73%	97 / 72%	96 / 71%	95 / 71%	94 / 70%	93 / 69%	92 / 68%	91 / 68%	90 / 67%
10011001	2	Durum wheat	100 / 74%	or 90 / 67%	10% / 9%	yes	99 / 73%	98 / 73%	97 / 72%	96 / 71%	95 / 71%	94 / 70%	93 / 69%	92 / 68%	91 / 68%	90 / 67%
		Coarse grains														
10059099	3	Maize	206 / 215%	or 185 / 194%	10%	yes	204 / 213%	202 / 211%	200 / 209%	198 / 207%	196 / 205%	193 / 202%	191 / 200%	189 / 198%	187 / 196%	185 / 194%
10030099	4	Barley	160 / 128%	or 144 / 115.2%	10%	yes	158 / 127%	157 / 125%	155 / 124%	154 / 123%	152 / 122%	150 / 120%	149 / 119%	147 / 118%	146 / 116%	144 / 115%
10040099	5	Oats	50	45	10%	yes	50	49	49	48	48	47	47	46	46	45
10061001	6	Rice	10	9	10%	yes	10	10	10	10	10	9	9	9	9	9
		Oilseeds														
12010002	7	Soyabeans	50	45	10%	yes	50	49	49	48	48	47	47	46	46	45
12050090	8	Rapeseed														
12060099	9	Sunflower	50	36	28%		49	47	46	44	43	42	40	39	37	36
		Sugar														
170111	10	Raw (cane) sugar	400 / 173%	or 360 / 156%	10%	yes	396 / 171%	392 / 170%	388 / 168%	384 / 166%	380 / 165%	376 / 163%	372 / 161%	368 / 159%	364 / 158%	360 / 156%
17019900	11	Refined sugar	400 / 173%	or 360 / 156%	10%	yes	396 / 171%	392 / 170%	388 / 168%	384 / 166%	380 / 165%	376 / 163%	372 / 161%	368 / 159%	364 / 158%	360 / 156%
		Milk														
04012000	12	Liquid milk (human cons.)	50	37.5	25%	yes	48.75	47.50	46.25	45.00	43.75	42.50	41.25	40.00	38.75	37.50
04021001	13	Skim milk powder	1 160 / 139%	or 1 044 / 125.1%	10%	yes	1 150 / 138%	1 140 / 136%	1 130 / 135%	1 110 / 133%	1 100 / 132%	1 090 / 131%	1 080 / 129%	1 070 / 128%	1 060 / 126%	1 040 / 125%
04050000	14	Butter	50	37.5	25%	yes	48.75	47.50	46.25	45.00	43.75	42.50	41.25	40.00	38.75	37.50
04069006	15	Cheese (Emmental)	50	45	10%	yes	49.50	49.00	48.50	48.00	47.50	47.00	46.50	46.00	45.50	45.00
		Beef and veal														
01029002	17	Live animals	10	9	10%		10	10	10	10	10	9	9	9	9	9
02021001	18	Beefmeat	50	45	10%		50	49	49	48	48	47	47	46	46	45
		Pigmeat														
02032101	19	Pigmeat	50	45	10%	yes	50	49	49	48	48	47	47	46	46	45
		Poultrymeat														
02071001	20	Poultrymeat	1 680 / 260%	or 1 512 / 234%	10%	yes	1 663 / 257%	1 646 / 255%	1 630 / 252%	1 613 / 250%	1 596 / 247%	1 579 / 244%	1 562 / 242%	1 546 / 239%	1 529 / 237%	1 512 / 234%
		Sheepmeat														
02042100	21	Lamb	25	22.5	10%	yes	24.75	24.50	24.25	24.00	23.75	23.50	23.25	23.00	22.75	22.50
51012100	22	Wool (< 75%)	10	9	10%		9.90	9.80	9.70	9.60	9.50	9.40	9.30	9.20	9.10	9.00
		Wool (> 75%)	50	37	26%		48.70	47.40	46.10	44.80	43.50	42.20	40.90	39.60	38.30	37.00
04070099	23	Eggs	50	37.5	25%	yes	48.75	47.50	46.25	45.00	43.75	42.50	41.25	40.00	38.75	37.50

1. Average of 1986-88.
2. Year of implementation of bound rate of duty = 2000.

Table III.11. **Export Subsidy Commitments, volumes and values: United States**[1]

Volumes (tonnes)	Average Base Level		Commitments		Additionality
	1986-90	1991-92	1995	2000	
Wheat ('000 tonnes)	18 382	21 449	20 236	14 522	7 492
Coarse grains ('000 tonnes)	1 975		1 906	1 561	
Rice	48 802	327 795	271 660	38 554	673 698
Vegetable oils	178 860	692 771	587 538	141 299	1 244 815
Butter & butter oils	26 705	47 863	42 989	21 097	51 656
Skim milk powder	86 331	116 871	108 227	68 201	74 753
Cheese	3 836	4 839	3 829	3 030	382
Other milk products	43	15 560	12 456	34	37 244
Beef	22 265		21 486	17 589	
Pigmeat	500		483	395	
Poultry	35 436		34 196	27 994	
Eggs ('000 dozens)	8 759	35 782	30 262	6 920	65 428

Values ('000 US$)	Average Base Level		Commitments		Additionality
	1986-90	1991-92	1995	2000	
Wheat	568 460	855 256	765 499	363 815	693 440
Coarse grains	72 059		67 735	46 118	
Rice	3 701	18 919	15 706	2 369	36 681
Vegetable oils	22 004	62 073	52 960	14 083	96 829
Butter & butter oil	47 652		44 793	30 497	
Skim milk powder	128 850		121 119	82 464	
Cheese	5 681		5 340	3 636	
Other milk products	33	17 961	14 374	21	43 029
Beef	35 660		33 520	22 822	
Pigmeat	777		730	497	
Poultry	22 742		21 377	14 555	
Eggs ('000 dozens)	2 507	9 009	7 588	1 604	15 694

Note: 1. If subsidised exports during the period 1986-90 were lower than those during the period 1991-92, the base period for reductions was generally the latter. **Additionality** means the increase in subsidised exports over the implementation period which results from the use of the 1991-92 base compared to the use of the 1986-90 base period.

Source: US Uruguay Round Schedule, GATT.

86

Table III.12. Export Subsidy Commitments, volumes and values: European Community[1]

Volumes ('000 tonnes)	Average Base Level		Commitments		Additionality
	1986-90	1991-92	1995	2000	
Wheat & flour	17 008	20 326.9	19 119	13 436	8 118
Coarse grains	12 624		12 182	9 973	
Rice	184		177	145	
Rapeseed	100		97	79	
Olive oil	148		143	117	
Sugar	1 617		1 560	1 277	
Butter & butter oil	463		447	366	
Skim milk powder	308		297	243	
Cheese	386	428	407	305	103
Other milk products	1 188	1 207.9	1 161.4	939	44.7
Beef meat	1 034	1 182.4	1 119	817	363
Pigmeat	509		491	402	
Poultry	368	472	440	290	255.3
Eggs	105	112.2	107.2	83	17.6
Wine	3 080		2 973	2 434	
Fruits & vegetables, fresh	1148		1 108	907	
Fruits & vegetables, preserved	201		194	159	
Raw tobacco	143	207	190.4	113	157
Alcohol	1 452		1 402	1 147	
Incorporated products	–	–			

Values (Ecu$ mn)	Average Base Level		Commitments		Additionality
	1986-90	1991-92	1995	2000	
Wheat & flour	1 783	2 273	2 069	1 141	1 180
Coarse grains	1 380		1 297	883	
Rice	62		58	40	
Rapeseed	32		30	21	
Olive oil	86		81	55	
Sugar	776		730	497	
Butter & butter oil	1 325		1 246	848	
Skim milk powder	370		348	237	
Cheese	439	554.4	505	281	277
Other milk products	1 008		947	645	
Beef meat	1 968	2 038.2	1 901	1 259	153
Pigmeat	183		172	117	
Poultry	143	147.8	138	92	9.4
Eggs	40		38	25	
Wine	65		61	41	
Fruits & vegetables, fresh	103		97	66	
Fruits & vegetables, preserved	15		15	10	
Raw tobacco	63	107.3	95	40	107.7
Alcohol	150		141	96	
Incorporated products	573		646	366	

1. See note (1) to Table III.11.
Source: EC Uruguay Round Schedule. GATT.

Table III.13. **Export Subsidy Commitments, volumes and values: Canada**[1]

Volumes ('000 tonnes)	Average Base Level		Commitments		Additionality
	1986-90	1991-92	1995	2000	
Wheat & wheat products	11 204.8	14 608	13 590.3	8 851.8	8 333
Coarse grains	4 579.2		4 418.9	3 617.6	
Oilseeds	2 214.1		2 136.7	1 749.2	
Butter	4.4	12.5	9.5	3.5	16
Skim milk powder	56.9		54.9	45	
Cheese	11.5	13	12.4	9.1	4
Other milk products	38.3		37	30.3	
Vegetable oil	117.4		113.3	92.8	
Oilcakes and meal	274.4		264.8	216.8	
Vegetables	101.4	258	224.5	80.1	380
Incorporated products					

Values (C$ mn)	Average Base Level		Commitments		Additionality
	1986-90	1991-92	1995	2000	
Wheat & wheat products	311.0	355	326.9	199.1	103.7
Coarse grains	116.4		109.4	74.5	
Oilseeds	59.7		56.1	38.2	
Butter	17.2	45.4	38.9	11.0	68.2
Skim milk powder	48.7		45.8	31.1	
Cheese	25.4	31.7	28.9	16.2	15
Other milk products	35.2		33.1	22.5	
Vegetable Oil	3.5		3.3	2.2	
Oilcakes and meal	7.5		7.0	4.8	
Vegetable Oil	3.1	6.3	5.5	2.0	7.7
Incorporated products	31.7	37.3	34.2	20.3	13.3

1. See note (1) to Table III.11.
Source: Canada Uruguay Round Schedule, GATT.

Table III.14. **Export Subsidy Commitments, volumes and values: Australia**[1]

Volumes (tonnes)	Average Base Level		Commitments		Additionality
	1986-90	1991-92	1995	2000	
Butter & butter oil	49 149	68 682	63 706	38 828	48 833
Skim milk powder	85 615	114 042	106 308	67 636	71 068
Cheese	63 139	76 421	71 997	49 880	33 205
Other milk products					
– Fats	16 527	21 376	19 989	13 056	12 123
– Solids non fats	64 017	96 520	88 862	50 573	82 258

Values (A$ mn)	Average Base Level		Commitments		Additionality
	1986-90	1991-92	1995	2000	
Butter & butter oil	22.44	26.40	24.39	14.36	9.90
Skim milk powder	37.15	41.40	38.46	23.78	10.63
Cheese	33.97	32.70	30.87	21.74	–3.17
Other milk products	43.74	44.70	41.92	27.99	2.40

1. See note (1) to Table III.11.
Source: Australian Uruguay Round Schedule, GATT.

Table III.15. **Export Subsidy Commitments, volumes and values: Switzerland**[1]

Volumes (tonnes)	Average Base Level		Commitments		Additionality
	1986-90	1991-92	1995	2000	
Milk products	78.68		75.94	62.16	
Potatoes	10.68		10.31	8.44	
Animals	14.31		13.81	11.3	
Fruit	12.0		11.58	9.48	

Values (SF mn)	Average Base Level		Commitments		Additionality
	1986-90	1991-92	1995	2000	
Milk products	443.7		417.08	284	
Potatoes	3.6		3.38	2.3	
Animals	35		32.9	22.4	
Fruit	26.2		24.55	16.8	
Processed products	179.6		168.82	114.9	

1. See note (1) to Table III.11.
Source: Swiss Uruguay Round Schedule, GATT.

Table III.16. **Export Subsidy Commitments, volumes and values: Norway**[1]

Volumes (tonnes)	Average Base Level		Commitments		Additionality
	1986-90	1991-92	1995	2000	
Bovine meat	1 895.2	3 610	3 257.9	1 497.2	4 287
Pigmeat	4 799		4 631	3 791.2	
Sheepmeat	861.6		8 31.4	680.7	
Poultry meat	28.4		27.4	22.4	
Egg & egg products	1 997		1 927.1	1 577.6	
Butter	7 433.8		7 173.6	5 872.7	
Cheese	20 515.8	24 333	22 978.7	16 207.5	9 543
Whey powder	30	143	123	23.7	282.5
Fruits & vegetables	841	1 577	1 424.9	644.4	1 840
Honey	18.2	54	47.4	14.4	89.5
Processed products					

Values (NKr mn)	Average Base Level		Commitments		Additionality
	1986-90	1991-92	1995	2000	
Bovine meat	54.6	115.7	102.3	35	152.8
Pigmeat	135.5		127.4	86.7	
Sheepmeat	27.6		25.9	17.7	
Poultry meat	0.74		0.70	0.47	
Egg & egg products	26.9		25.3	17.2	
Butter	83.2		78.2	53.2	
Cheese	384	596	537.6	245.8	530
Whey powder	0.04	5.3	4.4	0.025	13.2
Fruits & vegetables	0.9	1.5	1.3	0.56	1.6
Honey	0.12	0.7	0.6	0.077	1.5
Processed products	56.9		50.7	36.4	

1. See note (1) to Table III.11.
Source: Norwegian Uruguay Round Schedule, GATT.

Table III.17. **Export Subsidy Commitments,volumes and values: Iceland[1]**

Volumes (tonnes)	Average Base Level		Commitments		Additionality
	1986-90	1991-92	1995	2000	
Milk products (mn litres)	4		0	3.16	
Sheepmeat	2 275		0	1 797	

Values (SDR mn)	Average Base Level		Commitments		Additionality
	1986-90	1991-92	1995	2000	
Milk products	4.1		0	2.6	
Sheepmeat	14.5		0	9.3	

1. See note (1) to Table III.11.
Source: Iceland's Uruguay Round Schedule, GATT

Table III.18. **Export Subsidy Commitments, volumes and values: Mexico[1]**

Volumes ('000 tonnes)	Average Base Level		Commitments		Additionality
	1986-90	1990-91	1995	2004	
Wheat		402.6	395.3	332.1	
Maize		3 055.3	3 000	2 520	
Sorghum		522.5	513.1	431	
Sugar		1 527.7	1 500	1 260	
Kidney beans		172.3	169.2	142.1	

Values (US$ mn)	Average Base Level		Commitments		Additionality
	1986-90	1990-91	1995	2004	
Wheat		12.2	11.8	9	
Maize		139.3	135.5	102.9	
Sorghum		18	17.5	13.3	
Sugar		570.6	555	421.8	
Kidney beans		8.2	8	6.1	

1. See note (1) to Table III.11.
Source: Mexican Uruguay Round Schedule. GATT

COMPARISON OF TRENDS IN AMSs AND PSEs

The following graphs indicate the evolution since 1986 of the Aggregate Measurement of Support (AMS) and of the Producer Subsidy Equivalent (PSE) for a selected group of countries and commodities. The PSEs are calculated according to the usual definitions, as reported annually in the context of the annual Monitoring and Outlook Report. The AMSs for individual commodities have been updated, following the procedures and data outlined in the supporting tables to the country schedules. Both indicators have been expressed as indices with 1986=100. In many cases, the starting levels of PSE and AMS for a given commodity are significantly different in absolute terms. This reflects, inter alia, the fact that AMS is calculated using administered prices – and not producer prices as in the PSE – and fixed reference prices – whereas PSE uses a variable reference price.

Graph III.1 A comparison of trends in AMS and PSE: Common wheat
(Index 1986 =100)

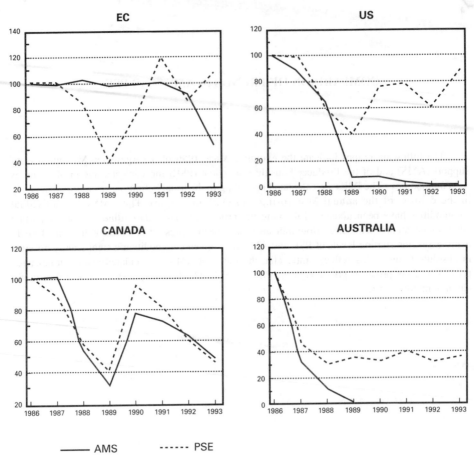

Note: Deficiency payments are included in the base period AMS of the United States but have not been included in years subsequent to 1988.

Source: OECD database, OECD secretariat estimates of current AMS levels.

Graph III.2 **A comparison of trends in AMS and PSE: Rice**
(Index 1986 = 100)

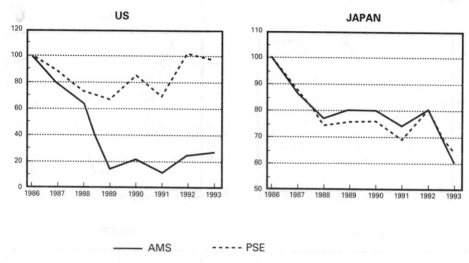

Note: Deficiency payments are included in the base period AMS of the United States but have not been included in years subsequent to 1988.

Source: OECD database, OECD secretariat estimates of current AMS levels.

Graph III.3 **A comparison of trends in AMS and PSE: Sugar**
(Index 1986 = 100)

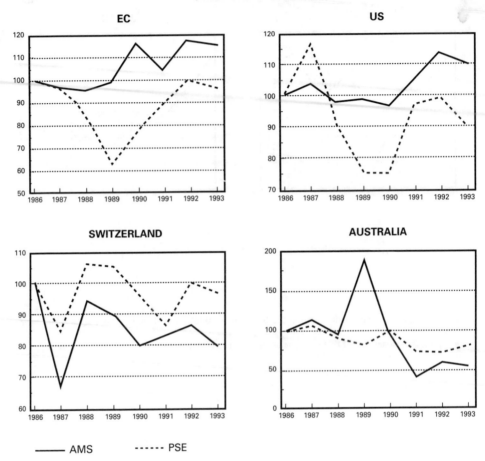

Source: OECD database, OECD secretariat estimates of current AMS levels.

Graph III.4 **A comparison of trends in AMS and PSE: Milk**
(Index 1986 = 100)

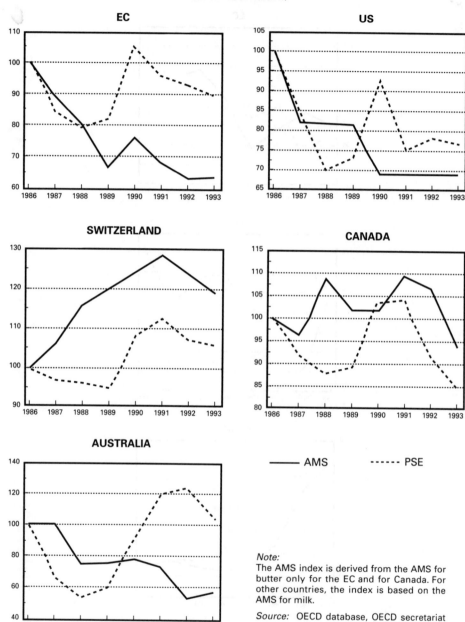

EC

US

SWITZERLAND

CANADA

AUSTRALIA

——— AMS   ----- PSE

Note:
The AMS index is derived from the AMS for butter only for the EC and for Canada. For other countries, the index is based on the AMS for milk.

Source: OECD database, OECD secretariat estimates of current AMS levels.

Graph III.5 A comparison of trends in AMS and PSE: Beef
(Index 1986 =100)

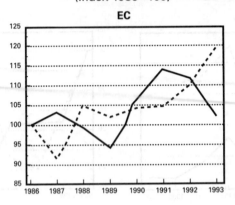

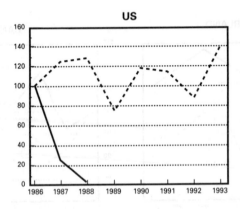

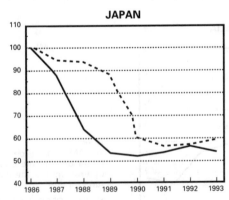

Source: OECD database, OECD secretariat estimates of current AMS levels.

MAIN SALES OUTLETS OF OECD PUBLICATIONS
PRINCIPAUX POINTS DE VENTE DES PUBLICATIONS DE L'OCDE

ARGENTINA – ARGENTINE
Carlos Hirsch S.R.L.
Galería Güemes, Florida 165, 4° Piso
1333 Buenos Aires   Tel. (1) 331.1787 y 331.2391
Telefax: (1) 331.1787

AUSTRALIA – AUSTRALIE
D.A. Information Services
648 Whitehorse Road, P.O.B 163
Mitcham, Victoria 3132   Tel. (03) 873.4411
Telefax: (03) 873.5679

AUSTRIA – AUTRICHE
Gerold & Co.
Graben 31
Wien I   Tel. (0222) 533.50.14
Telefax: (0222) 512.47.31.29

BELGIUM – BELGIQUE
Jean De Lannoy
Avenue du Roi 202 Koningslaan
B-1060 Bruxelles   Tel. (02) 538.51.69/538.08.41
Telefax: (02) 538.08.41

CANADA
Renouf Publishing Company Ltd.
1294 Algoma Road
Ottawa, ON K1B 3W8   Tel. (613) 741.4333
Telefax: (613) 741.5439
Stores:
61 Sparks Street
Ottawa, ON K1P 5R1   Tel. (613) 238.8985
211 Yonge Street
Toronto, ON M5B 1M4   Tel. (416) 363.3171
Telefax: (416)363.59.63

Les Éditions La Liberté Inc.
3020 Chemin Sainte-Foy
Sainte-Foy, PQ G1X 3V6   Tel. (418) 658.3763
Telefax: (418) 658.3763

Federal Publications Inc.
165 University Avenue, Suite 701
Toronto, ON M5H 3B8   Tel. (416) 860.1611
Telefax: (416) 860.1608

Les Publications Fédérales
1185 Université
Montréal, QC H3B 3A7   Tel. (514) 954.1633
Telefax: (514) 954.1635

CHINA – CHINE
China National Publications Import
Export Corporation (CNPIEC)
16 Gongti E. Road, Chaoyang District
P.O. Box 88 or 50
Beijing 100704 PR   Tel. (01) 506.6688
Telefax: (01) 506.3101

CHINESE TAIPEI – TAIPEI CHINOIS
Good Faith Worldwide Int'l. Co. Ltd.
9th Floor, No. 118, Sec. 2
Chung Hsiao E. Road
Taipei   Tel. (02) 391.7396/391.7397
Telefax: (02) 394.9176

CZECH REPUBLIC – RÉPUBLIQUE TCHÈQUE
Artia Pegas Press Ltd.
Narodni Trida 25
POB 825
111 21 Praha 1   Tel. 26.65.68
Telefax: 26.20.81

DENMARK – DANEMARK
Munksgaard Book and Subscription Service
35, Nørre Søgade, P.O. Box 2148
DK-1016 København K   Tel. (33) 12.85.70
Telefax: (33) 12.93.87

EGYPT – ÉGYPTE
Middle East Observer
41 Sherif Street
Cairo   Tel. 392.6919
Telefax: 360-6804

FINLAND – FINLANDE
Akateeminen Kirjakauppa
Keskuskatu 1, P.O. Box 128
00100 Helsinki
Subscription Services/Agence d'abonnements :
P.O. Box 23
00371 Helsinki   Tel. (358 0) 121 4416
Telefax: (358 0) 121.4450

FRANCE
OECD/OCDE
Mail Orders/Commandes par correspondance:
2, rue André-Pascal
75775 Paris Cedex 16   Tel. (33-1) 45.24.82.00
Telefax: (33-1) 49.10.42.76
Telex: 640048 OCDE
Internet: Compte.PUBSINQ @ oecd.org
Orders via Minitel, France only/
Commandes par Minitel, France exclusivement :
36 15 OCDE

OECD Bookshop/Librairie de l'OCDE :
33, rue Octave-Feuillet
75016 Paris   Tel. (33-1) 45.24.81.81
(33-1) 45.24.81.67

Documentation Française
29, quai Voltaire
75007 Paris   Tel. 40.15.70.00

Gibert Jeune (Droit-Économie)
6, place Saint-Michel
75006 Paris   Tel. 43.25.91.19

Librairie du Commerce International
10, avenue d'Iéna
75016 Paris   Tel. 40.73.34.60

Librairie Dunod
Université Paris-Dauphine
Place du Maréchal de Lattre de Tassigny
75016 Paris   Tel. (1) 44.05.40.13

Librairie Lavoisier
11, rue Lavoisier
75008 Paris   Tel. 42.65.39.95

Librairie L.G.D.J. - Montchrestien
20, rue Soufflot
75005 Paris   Tel. 46.33.89.85

Librairie des Sciences Politiques
30, rue Saint-Guillaume
75007 Paris   Tel. 45.48.36.02

P.U.F.
49, boulevard Saint-Michel
75005 Paris   Tel. 43.25.83.40

Librairie de l'Université
12a, rue Nazareth
13100 Aix-en-Provence   Tel. (16) 42.26.18.08

Documentation Française
165, rue Garibaldi
69003 Lyon   Tel. (16) 78.63.32.23

Librairie Decitre
29, place Bellecour
69002 Lyon   Tel. (16) 72.40.54.54

Librairie Sauramps
Le Triangle
34967 Montpellier Cedex 2 Tel. (16) 67.58.85.15
Tekefax: (16) 67.58.27.36

GERMANY – ALLEMAGNE
OECD Publications and Information Centre
August-Bebel-Allee 6
D-53175 Bonn   Tel. (0228) 959.120
Telefax: (0228) 959.12.17

GREECE – GRÈCE
Librairie Kauffmann
Mavrokordatou 9
106 78 Athens   Tel. (01) 32.55.321
Telefax: (01) 32.30.320

HONG-KONG
Swindon Book Co. Ltd.
Astoria Bldg. 3F
34 Ashley Road, Tsimshatsui
Kowloon, Hong Kong   Tel. 2376.2062
Telefax: 2376.0685

HUNGARY – HONGRIE
Euro Info Service
Margitsziget, Európa Ház
1138 Budapest   Tel. (1) 111.62.16
Telefax: (1) 111.60.61

ICELAND – ISLANDE
Mál Mog Menning
Laugavegi 18, Pósthólf 392
121 Reykjavik   Tel. (1) 552.4240
Telefax: (1) 562.3523

INDIA – INDE
Oxford Book and Stationery Co.
Scindia House
New Delhi 110001   Tel. (11) 331.5896/5308
Telefax: (11) 332.5993

17 Park Street
Calcutta 700016   Tel. 240832

INDONESIA – INDONÉSIE
Pdii-Lipi
P.O. Box 4298
Jakarta 12042   Tel. (21) 573.34.67
Telefax: (21) 573.34.67

IRELAND – IRLANDE
Government Supplies Agency
Publications Section
4/5 Harcourt Road
Dublin 2   Tel. 661.31.11
Telefax: 475.27.60

ISRAEL
Praedicta
5 Shatner Street
P.O. Box 34030
Jerusalem 91430   Tel. (2) 52.84.90/1/2
Telefax: (2) 52.84.93

R.O.Y. International
P.O. Box 13056
Tel Aviv 61130   Tel. (3) 546 1423
Telefax: (3) 546 1442

Palestinian Authority/Middle East:
INDEX Information Services
P.O.B. 19502
Jerusalem   Tel. (2) 27.12.19
Telefax: (2) 27.16.34

ITALY – ITALIE
Libreria Commissionaria Sansoni
Via Duca di Calabria 1/1
50125 Firenze   Tel. (055) 64.54.15
Telefax: (055) 64.12.57

Via Bartolini 29
20155 Milano   Tel. (02) 36.50.83

Editrice e Libreria Herder
Piazza Montecitorio 120
00186 Roma   Tel. 679.46.28
Telefax: 678.47.51

Libreria Hoepli
Via Hoepli 5
20121 Milano   Tel. (02) 86.54.46
Telefax: (02) 805.28.86

Libreria Scientifica
Dott. Lucio de Biasio 'Aeiou'
Via Coronelli, 6
20146 Milano   Tel. (02) 48.95.45.52
Telefax: (02) 48.95.45.48

JAPAN – JAPON
OECD Publications and Information Centre
Landic Akasaka Building
2-3-4 Akasaka, Minato-ku
Tokyo 107   Tel. (81.3) 3586.2016
Telefax: (81.3) 3584.7929

KOREA – CORÉE
Kyobo Book Centre Co. Ltd.
P.O. Box 1658, Kwang Hwa Moon
Seoul   Tel. 730.78.91
Telefax: 735.00.30

MALAYSIA – MALAISIE
University of Malaya Bookshop
University of Malaya
P.O. Box 1127, Jalan Pantai Baru
59700 Kuala Lumpur
Malaysia   Tel. 756.5000/756.5425
                               Telefax: 756.3246

MEXICO – MEXIQUE
Revistas y Periodicos Internacionales S.A. de C.V.
Florencia 57 - 1004
Mexico, D.F. 06600   Tel. 207.81.00
                               Telefax: 208.39.79

NETHERLANDS – PAYS-BAS
SDU Uitgeverij Plantijnstraat
Externe Fondsen
Postbus 20014
2500 EA's-Gravenhage   Tel. (070) 37.89.880
Voor bestellingen: Telefax: (070) 34.75.778

NEW ZEALAND
NOUVELLE-ZÉLANDE
GPLegislation Services
P.O. Box 12418
Thorndon, Wellington   Tel. (04) 496.5655
                               Telefax: (04) 496.5698

NORWAY – NORVÈGE
Narvesen Info Center – NIC
Bertrand Narvesens vei 2
P.O. Box 6125 Etterstad
0602 Oslo 6   Tel. (022) 57.33.00
                               Telefax: (022) 68.19.01

PAKISTAN
Mirza Book Agency
65 Shahrah Quaid-E-Azam
Lahore 54000   Tel. (42) 353.601
                               Telefax: (42) 231.730

PHILIPPINE – PHILIPPINES
International Book Center
5th Floor, Filipinas Life Bldg.
Ayala Avenue
Metro Manila   Tel. 81.96.76
                           Telex 23312 RHP PH

PORTUGAL
Livraria Portugal
Rua do Carmo 70-74
Apart. 2681
1200 Lisboa   Tel. (01) 347.49.82/5
                              Telefax: (01) 347.02.64

SINGAPORE – SINGAPOUR
Gower Asia Pacific Pte Ltd.
Golden Wheel Building
41, Kallang Pudding Road, No. 04-03
Singapore 1334   Tel. 741.5166
                               Telefax: 742.9356

SPAIN – ESPAGNE
Mundi-Prensa Libros S.A.
Castelló 37, Apartado 1223
Madrid 28001   Tel. (91) 431.33.99
                              Telefax: (91) 575.39.98

Libreria Internacional AEDOS
Consejo de Ciento 391
08009 – Barcelona   Tel. (93) 488.30.09
                             Telefax: (93) 487.76.59

Llibreria de la Generalitat
Palau Moja
Rambla dels Estudis, 118
08002 – Barcelona
              (Subscripcions) Tel. (93) 318.80.12
              (Publicacions) Tel. (93) 302.67.23
                            Telefax: (93) 412.18.54

SRI LANKA
Centre for Policy Research
c/o Colombo Agencies Ltd.
No. 300-304, Galle Road
Colombo 3   Tel. (1) 574240, 573551-2
                     Telefax: (1) 575394, 510711

SWEDEN – SUÈDE
Fritzes Customer Service
S–106 47 Stockholm   Tel. (08) 690.90.90
                             Telefax: (08) 20.50.21

Subscription Agency/Agence d'abonnements :
Wennergren-Williams Info AB
P.O. Box 1305
171 25 Solna   Tel. (08) 705.97.50
                             Telefax: (08) 27.00.71

SWITZERLAND – SUISSE
Maditec S.A. (Books and Periodicals - Livres
et périodiques)
Chemin des Palettes 4
Case postale 266
1020 Renens VD 1   Tel. (021) 635.08.65
                            Telefax: (021) 635.07.80

Librairie Payot S.A.
4, place Pépinet
CP 3212
1002 Lausanne   Tel. (021) 341.33.47
                            Telefax: (021) 341.33.45

Librairie Unilivres
6, rue de Candolle
1205 Genève   Tel. (022) 320.26.23
                            Telefax: (022) 329.73.18

Subscription Agency/Agence d'abonnements :
Dynapresse Marketing S.A.
38 avenue Vibert
1227 Carouge   Tel. (022) 308.07.89
                            Telefax: (022) 308.07.99

See also – Voir aussi :
OECD Publications and Information Centre
August-Bebel-Allee 6
D-53175 Bonn (Germany)   Tel. (0228) 959.120
                            Telefax: (0228) 959.12.17

THAILAND – THAÏLANDE
Suksit Siam Co. Ltd.
113, 115 Fuang Nakhon Rd.
Opp. Wat Rajbopith
Bangkok 10200   Tel. (662) 225.9531/2
                            Telefax: (662) 222.5188

TURKEY – TURQUIE
Kültür Yayinlari Is-Türk Ltd. Sti.
Atatürk Bulvari No. 191/Kat 13
Kavaklidere/Ankara   Tel. 428.11.40 Ext. 2458
Dolmabahce Cad. No. 29
Besiktas/Istanbul   Tel. (312) 260 7188
                            Telex: (312) 418 29 46

UNITED KINGDOM – ROYAUME-UNI
HMSO
Gen. enquiries   Tel. (171) 873 8496
Postal orders only:
P.O. Box 276, London SW8 5DT
Personal Callers HMSO Bookshop
49 High Holborn, London WC1V 6HB
                            Telefax: (171) 873 8416
Branches at: Belfast, Birmingham, Bristol,
Edinburgh, Manchester

UNITED STATES – ÉTATS-UNIS
OECD Publications and Information Center
2001 L Street N.W., Suite 650
Washington, D.C. 20036-4910 Tel. (202) 785.6323
                            Telefax: (202) 785.0350

VENEZUELA
Libreria del Este
Avda F. Miranda 52, Aptdo. 60337
Edificio Galipán
Caracas 106   Tel. 951.1705/951.2307/951.1297
                       Telegram: Libreste Caracas

Subscription to OECD periodicals may also be
placed through main subscription agencies.

Les abonnements aux publications périodiques de
l'OCDE peuvent être souscrits auprès des
principales agences d'abonnement.

Orders and inquiries from countries where Distribu-
tors have not yet been appointed should be sent to:
OECD Publications Service, 2 rue André-Pascal,
75775 Paris Cedex 16, France.

Les commandes provenant de pays où l'OCDE n'a
pas encore désigné de distributeur peuvent être
adressées à : OCDE, Service des Publications,
2, rue André-Pascal, 75775 Paris Cedex 16, France.

7-1995

OECD PUBLICATIONS, 2 rue André-Pascal, 75775 PARIS CEDEX 16
PRINTED IN FRANCE
(51 95 13 1) ISBN 92-64-14582-6 - No. 48221 1995